Decorating Eggs

To Buddy

Decorating Eggs

Exquisite Designs
with Wax & Dye

Jane Pollak

Sterling Publishing Co., Inc.   New York
A Sterling/Lark Book

Editor: Bobbe Needham

Art Director and Production: Elaine Thompson

Photography: Evan Bracken

**Library of Congress Cataloging-in-Publication
Available**

10 9 8 7 6 5 4

A Sterling/Lark Book

First paperback edition published in 1998 by
  Sterling Publishing Company, Inc.
  387 Park Avenue South, New York, N.Y. 10016

Produced by Altamont Press, Inc.
  50 College Street, Asheville, NC 28801

© 1996 by Jane Pollak

Distributed in Canada by Sterling Publishing
  ℅ Canadian Manda Group, One Atlantic Avenue, Suite 105
  Toronto, Ontario, Canada M6K 3E7

Distributed in Great Britain and Europe by Cassell PLC
  Wellington House, 125 Strand, London WC2R 0BB, England

Distributed in Australia by Capricorn Link (Australia) Pty Ltd.
  P.O. Box 6651, Baulkham Hills, Business Centre, NSW 2153, Australia

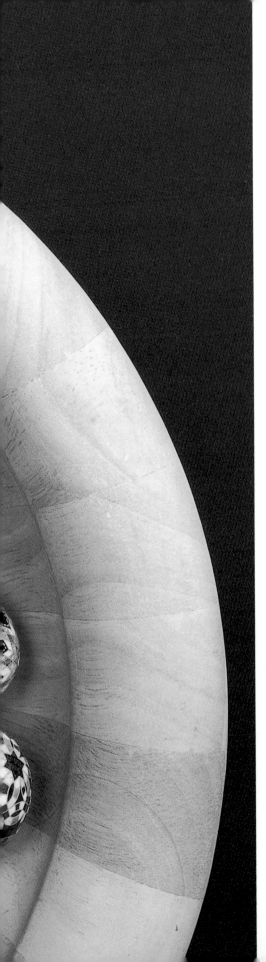

Contents

Chapter One

Introduction: My Father's Egg

I can't remember exactly how old I was, but I had to stand on tiptoe to see the top of my father's bureau, where he kept the things he most honored. Along with portrait photographs of my mother, grandmother, and grandfather, there sat a Ukrainian Easter egg, the first I had ever seen. My father handled special events for a department store, and a man who had spent the day in the store window showing people how to decorate these eggs had given him this one as a gift. He had brought it home and shown it to us with reverence, then given it a position of honor on his bureau, where I stood on tiptoe to look at it time and again. The wonder of it!...nestled in its brass holder, like an egg in a bird cage...but a bright, intricately patterned, multicolored egg, more beautiful than any Easter egg I had ever imagined.

Fast forward about twenty years, to 1972. I had begun teaching art at Westhill High School in Stamford, Connecticut, and needed some ideas for my class in art foundations, which focused on crafts. A colleague, Dorothy Discko, said she had enjoyed great success the previous year teaching students about Ukrainian Easter eggs. In my arrogance and ignorance as a fledgling teacher I thought, "Easter eggs in high school? How babyish!" To be polite, I asked her to show me what she was referring to. With that she opened up an egg carton filled with exquisitely designed and colored eggs. "How do you do that? Teach me!" I said. Dot showed me how to use a kistka, the stylus that one loads with wax to "write" on the egg, and with a brief demonstration and explanation she taught me the basics of the craft that has held me in its thrall for more than twenty years.

An egg carton full of traditional Ukrainian Easter eggs—a visual feast.

For my first Ukrainian Easter egg, I used food coloring from the grocery store, combined with lots of enthusiasm.

Dot gave me my first kistka that day. I stopped at the hardware store on my way home and bought a one-pound brick of beeswax (which lasted me for the next ten years). That same night I created my first Ukrainian Easter egg using food coloring for dye. It combined my two favorite elements of art—line and color. I thought it was the most beautiful creation of my life and believed I had found my art form.

When I introduced Ukrainian Easter eggs to my students that year, they took to the craft with such enthusiasm that I wrote a note to a journalist at the *New York Times*, who came out with a photographer to write an article about our class. My students had added their own twist to this ancient art, using the egg as a canvas and creating everything from ladybugs to a pair of Adidas sneakers.

One of the Ukrainian eggs I designed for this book, built around a traditional oak-leaf pattern.

During my two years at Westhill, I made frequent trips to the Ukrainian section of New York City for dyes, beeswax, kistkas, and books. My favorite shop was Surma, partly because Mr. Surmach, whose family owned the store, always greeted me warmly on the phone or in person. Over one springtime school vacation, I decided to buy a hand-embroidered Ukrainian blouse to wear for an egg-decorating demonstration I would be giving at the invitation of a store in lower Manhattan. As I looked through the selection at Surma, I chatted with Mr. Surmach about this opportunity. He told me that he used to sit in the window of a department store on Forty-second Street each year and decorate one egg after another. I asked which store. "Stern Brothers," he replied.

"My father used to work there," I said. "Did you ever know Larry Goodman?"

"Of course," he said. "He hired me to do the demonstrations. I gave him one of my eggs."

❖

Back in 1973 the handcraft movement in the United States was just beginning to gather steam. In the New England community where I lived, the Pink Tent Festival, held every summer, gave artists the opportunity to sell their wares. Equipped with a card table and a few dozen eggs, I set up my first craft booth at the Pink Tent. To my amazement people other than my relatives and friends actually parted with eight dollars for one of my decorated eggs packaged in half an egg carton. And Bloomingdale's special-events director happened by and asked if I would run a one-day program at the store. This began to look like an easy way to make a living. Just show up with your work, and opportunities happen. I have since learned the phrase "uninformed optimism," which is a cousin of beginner's luck.

More than twenty years have passed since that festival. My perspective has changed. Being a full-time craft artist is a constant challenge balanced by the pleasure of working with my hands in a medium that I find endlessly intriguing. I have traveled coast to coast to present my work and demonstrate my art form. At some shows I have sold thousands of dollars worth of pieces; on some days I have sold nothing. Some museum shops and catalogs offer my eggs and my jewelry made from eggshells—about an equal number of companies have rejected them. All in all, I would not have traded a minute for work in any other field. My work with the eggs has brought me to where I am today, which is exactly where I need to be.

✦

Eggs—and decorated eggs—combine the comfortably familiar with a mystique that has fascinated people since early time. Ancient peoples believed that the universe and all living things were created from a "great cosmic egg," write the authors of *Pysanka: Icon of the Universe*. By decorating symbols of this primal egg with images of "fertility, power, and life," these people believed they were helping the world stay "alive, powerful, and above all, good. Hence, the egg came to symbolize the greatest of all mysteries...the Mystery of Life."

Cultures in every corner of the earth have incorporated this symbol of rebirth into their rituals, folklore, and folk art. A Chinese myth tells us that the first man, Puonsu, emerged from an egg. Similarly, the Navajos believe that the Great Coyote Who Was Formed in the Water hatched from an egg. Jews around the world include a roasted egg on their Seder plates, part of the celebration of the Jews' release from Egypt into a new, free life. And the Ukrainians created the art form pysanka to decorate the egg and commemorate its talismanic powers.

The custom of exchanging dyed eggs began with the ancient Egyptians and Persians, although dyeing eggs for Easter probably dates to the Middle Ages, when the Eastern Orthodox faithful celebrated Christ's resurrection by placing dyed and jewel-bedecked eggs in a symbolic tomb and exchanged red-dyed eggs on Easter morning. In some Christian countries, eating eggs was forbidden during Lent. Chickens continued to lay eggs daily, of course, so families with hens accumulated large quantities of them. Giving the eggs away, also in great quantities, became associated with the celebration of Easter. The joy of creating and exchanging decorated eggs during this season continues, vastly commercialized, of course. At Easter, newspapers and magazines abound with articles on how to decorate eggs, and supermarkets feature eye-catching displays of egg-decorating kits. According to Dave Bowden, national egg supervisor of the *USDA Poultry Market News*, U.S. egg sales rise nearly 30 percent in the weeks before Easter.

✦

One winter, I received a personal awakening about the abundance—or lack of abundance—of eggs, which I had become complacent about seeing at the supermarket from January through December. After taking orders for eggshell jewelry at a show in February, I rushed back to my studio and called my supplier for a shipment of a hundred duck eggs so that I could start working immediately. The ducks, I was told, would not begin to lay eggs until early April. I was stunned. As long as I'd worked with eggs, taking nature into account hadn't occurred to me. I had to postpone all of my orders.

The ancient tradition of decorating and exchanging eggs in the springtime continues in many parts of the world, including the United States, where Easter baskets are big business.

Chapter Two

Eggs, Et Cetera: What You Need to Create Exquisite Eggs

What most of us call Ukrainian Easter eggs are in fact only one variety of decorated eggs more formally called *pysanka*. The plural—more than one pysanka—is *pysanky*. *Pysanka* is a Ukrainian word meaning "an egg that has been written on." The writing is done with molten wax to block out areas on the egg that will not be dyed. Through a succession of wax applications and different-colored dye baths, you can draw (or "write") simple or intricate patterns on the egg's surface. A more common word for this process is *batik*. Throughout this book I use the words *pysanky* and *batik* interchangeably to describe decorated eggs (in the chapter on Ukrainian Easter eggs, you'll see that this type is distinguished by particular designs and combinations of color).

Before you decorate your own eggs, it may require a slight mental twist to understand how the process works, because the design focus is on the areas not covered with wax. To draw a picture on paper, you usually begin with a black pencil or ink outline of the object. With batik eggs, the first wax lines you draw on the egg will always stay white—the color of the shell. They will appear as white outlines on the completed egg.

All kinds of surprises can happen as an egg goes through the series of dye baths. For instance, if you dip an egg you have dyed turquoise into yellow dye for just a moment, it will turn green—just what you would expect if you mixed turquoise and yellow paint. But if you let the turquoise egg sit in the yellow dye for several minutes, it will become totally yellow.

Once you've decorated a few of your own eggs, I think you'll find the process far more fascinating and fun than intimidating or mysterious. For several years I ran an after-school art program in my community for elementary-school children. One of our projects was making pysanky, which they adored. The children were totally uninhibited in their use of the dyes. I often had to ask them how they got a particular color, because it was one I had never seen. Typically they would say, "Oh. I put the purple egg into the orange dye." I would never have tried that, because anyone knows a light color like orange would never cover the purple. When my son began the craft, he used the egg to make statements like "Let's go, Mets!" in wax and dye. And they were beautiful too. (I recommend that children have a healthy respect for fire before you allow them to attempt this craft, usually around age eight or nine.)

I urge you to play with the tools and dyes, experiment with dye progressions, and ask a child to join you. Whether drawn with the scribbled abandon of a young child, the tentative lines of a beginning artist, or the intricate, detailed designs of a master, transforming a solid white shell into a multicolored wonder appeals to the artist in everyone.

THE EGG

Oh, acid rain and commercial chicken coops, what you have done to our egg supply! I imagine that a hundred years ago, eggshells were wonderfully thick and hard. Friends tell of grandmothers who raised their own chickens and bragged about how you had to really smash those shells on the cast-iron fryer to crack them open. Years and years of forcing chickens to lay eggs day and night, of boxing them up and feeding them antibiotics, has resulted not only in unhappy chickens but in eggshells of poorer quality. Traditionally, Ukrainians finished their decorated eggs not by hollowing them out, as we do today, but by allowing them to air dry for a year. Only a small percentage of today's supermarket eggs could endure that process. After several weeks, the thin shells begin to ooze, discolor, or—at worst—explode.

For pysanky, the ideal egg has a very smooth shell and as uniform and pleasing a shape as possible. When you begin to pay attention to shell quality, you'll notice every lump, wrinkle, and "pimple" on the egg surface. You'll become aware that *egg-shaped* can cover a lot of variety, from round to oblong. In general, I look for a pleasing, traditional egg shape.

For many years I drove to Walter Golden's farm in a neighboring Connecticut town to buy my eggs. Here the chickens were allowed to run free and were fed with chemical-free grains. The shells from their eggs were a joy to work on—smooth and thick, they dyed evenly. Mr. Golden selected my weekly order by hand, which gave both of us great pleasure. During the course of one of our exchanges, I was intrigued to learn that the size and age of a hen determine the size of her eggs—Mr. Golden told me that old hens produced the biggest, thickest-shelled eggs. Over the years, however, as the farm's wholesale customers called for more and more brown eggs, my supply of local farm-fresh white eggs diminished. (The wholesalers' customers perceived brown eggs as healthier and more natural than white ones—as in brown bread and brown rice. In fact, there is no difference nutritionally.)

This series of eggs is the work of surgeon Daniel Saracynski.

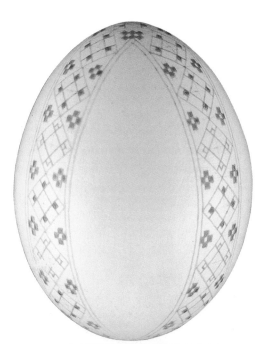

Today when I select eggs for decorating, I look for organic or cholesterol-monitored white eggs. They seem to have the most even shapes and the best shell quality, and to dye the most evenly.

In my years of egg decorating, and for the eggs in this book, I have mainly worked with white eggshells, which must be used if a color scheme includes pure-white lines or areas. You can produce any design on a brown egg as well, and the color gives the finished egg an almost antique quality that can be very beautiful and in some cases preferable. In some paisley designs, I prefer the look of the brown egg.

Egg size need not be a consideration, except in terms of practicality and preference. Over the years I have used almost every conceivable size of egg, from parakeet to ostrich. Although the variety you can work with may differ from country to country, the kinds of eggs I know are available in the United States are chicken, duck, goose, parakeet, cockatiel, and ostrich.

You will find a range of egg sizes to choose from—shown here are cockatiel, hen, duck, goose, and ostrich.

Of these, my favorites are the duck egg and the ostrich egg. Duck eggs have the best-dyeing, smoothest, and most beautiful shells. I recommend them for eggshell jewelry. Ostrich eggs present a challenge logistically—they don't fit nicely into most dye jars, they are literally a handful to work on, and they have a dimpled surface where dye collects and creates darker areas. I have fully decorated only a few ostrich eggs, each of which took an enormously long time to complete. I've also made bowls and barrettes from these shells (for an ostrich egg decorated and cut into a bowl shape, see page 115).

For most of the projects in this book, the focus will be on the humble grocery or health-food store variety Grade A hen egg.

Finally, about egg storage. If you don't intend to use the eggs within a few weeks, you may refrigerate them. But when I buy eggs for decorating, I immediately bring them into my studio so they will be ready to use at a moment's notice—they must be at room temperature for the wax to adhere. I occasionally lose one or two to thin-shell syndrome, and sometimes the two- or three-week wait in my studio lessens the dyeing quality, but I'd rather throw a couple away than have to postpone the creative urge while I wait for a refrigerated egg to warm to room temperature. It is never a good idea to artificially warm an egg either. Nature seems to know.

THE KISTKA

The Ukrainian word *kistka* translates to "chicken bone," which is probably what Ukrainians at first used to transfer heated wax onto the eggshell in making pysanky. Today, the word refers to a tool with a small funnel that allows bits of beeswax to be fed into a metallic well. When the well is heated, wax flows out a small opening at the opposite end onto the surface of the egg. Kistkas come in a variety of materials and sizes. All allow molten wax to flow out in a line, like ink from a pen.

Kistkas range from the inexpensive and somewhat primitive to the sleek, extra-fine electric versions. The low price of the simpler tools makes them ideal for anyone who wants simply to experiment with the craft; they do a fine job of melting the wax and getting it onto the egg. Compared to the electric tools, though, they are available only in thicker points, and they tend to drip unexpectedly and to produce somewhat uneven lines. For those preferring more control and detail in their egg decorating, I strongly recommend the deluxe brass-headed tools or the electric tools. If you can't wait to get started and don't want to break the bank, a fine-point deluxe brass hand tool for under five dollars will serve very well.

In my studio, I keep three electric kistkas plugged in and ready to go—an extra-fine, a medium, and a heavy point. There are electric tools available with interchangeable points, but you have to let the tool cool down to change the point and then wait for it to heat up again. As much patience as people assume this intricate craft requires, I hate waiting unnecessarily. And having three tools plugged in eliminates that delay. I also have several brass-headed tools and a few with aluminum heads that I use most often for filling in large areas of the egg with wax.

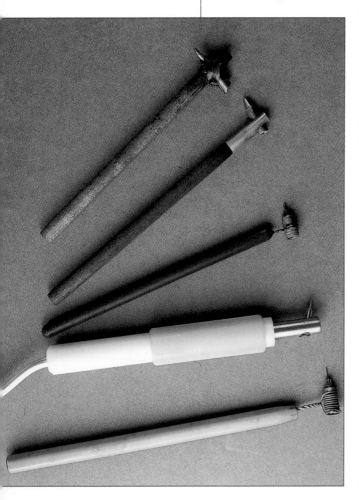

A variety of kistkas, from top: (1) An inexpensive, basic tool of wood, brass, and copper; (2) A good inexpensive beginner tool, whose molded aluminum head provides a more consistent line; (3) A deluxe tool with a beautifully crafted brass head and easy-to-hold handle; (4) A time-saving electric kistka that keeps the wax liquid; (5) A tool handcrafted by surgeon Daniel Saraczynski.

Slight differences in the way the dyes color an egg occur with brown eggs. These eggs were created by my friend Dorothy Discko.

*I designed this ostrich-egg ornament,
by invitation, for President Clinton's
White House Christmas tree in 1993.*

I keep a variety of different-size tips ready for use. For outlining I prefer an extra-fine tip, which allows the greatest intricacy. (The fine tip on the electric tool works better for ostrich eggs, as the extra-fine is actually too thin to hold a clear line.) Medium and heavy tips are excellent for filling in areas and can also be used for line work.

BEESWAX

The only wax to use for this craft is 100 percent pure beeswax. Widely available from hardware stores, notions departments in fabric stores, and hobby shops, a cake that will last through a couple of dozen eggs costs less than a dollar. Compared to paraffin, beeswax heats to a higher temperature, draws a finer line on the shell, and adheres better to the surface.

As one heats a nonelectric kistka over a flame, carbon will eventually blacken the tool and the wax around it. Blackened wax has the advantage of rendering the lines drawn on the egg easier to see as more dyes are applied. When using an electric tool, since there is no flame, no carbon accumulates, and the light-colored wax becomes progressively harder to see during the dyeing process. It is possible to buy beeswax already blackened, but the disadvantage of commercially blackened wax is that it tends to clog tools. If you prefer using an electric kistka, you can create your own darkened wax for it: Hold a nonelectric kistka in the flame, allow the carbon to build up, and then wipe it onto the cake of wax (as would naturally happen in the process with a nonelectric tool)—then go on to use this blackened wax in your electric kistka.

DYES

The frustrating aspect of dyeing eggs with food coloring is waiting for the results. My first egg took at least twenty minutes to turn pale blue. Aniline dyes, in contrast, are not only brilliant but fast acting. What took me twenty minutes with food coloring requires fewer than twenty seconds with aniline dyes.

Aniline dyes are chemically produced. At stores that sell Ukrainian Easter egg decorating supplies, they come powdered and prepackaged to the correct amount for mixing. Besides the traditional yellow, orange, red, green, and black, aniline dyes—just for starters—come in

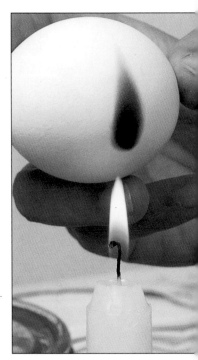

Carbon rises from the candle flame, blackening whatever is in its path—kistka, beeswax, or eggshell.

Beeswax comes in one-pound bricks or small blocks, either natural or blackened. For convenience, try making blackened wax snakes: blacken the wax with a carbon-stained kistka, gouge out small pieces with a small knife (as shown here), and roll them together to form a long coil.   Feed the wax snake into the kistka well as needed.

Aniline dyes work best for this craft. The powdered dyes are combined with vinegar and stored in glass jars with rubber rings, to preserve the dyes' freshness.

varying shades of blue from turquoise to royal and in bright pink, purple, and brown. They have a long shelf life in the powdered form, although each color has its own life span when mixed with water. Turquoise and purple, for instance, retain their intensity for years, while orange may need to be thrown out after only a few weeks.

Traditionally, dyes were derived from natural materials such as tree bark, berries, and onion skins, which produce beautiful muted shades when compared to the more vivid colors the aniline dyes create. Natural or vegetable dyes are also available through egg-decorating suppliers in premeasured, packaged amounts. Their color range, narrower than the analines', includes yellow, orange, red, blue, and black.

For egg decorating, one mixes aniline or vegetable dyes with boiling water in glass jars in the amount specified on the package. Glass is preferable for mixing and storing dyes because plastic will interact with the dyes' chemicals and alter the dye properties. (When working on an ostrich egg, I sometimes pour the dyes briefly into a large plastic container, dye the egg, and then pour the dyes back into the glass jar for storage—but only because it is easier to find plastic bowls than glass jars large enough to accommodate an ostrich egg and the chance of breakage is less.)

Almost all the colors require the addition of vinegar, which acts as a mordant for the dye. A mordant is the substance that allows the color to penetrate the surface of the shell. With some colors, such as orange, package directions specifically say not to use vinegar, as it interferes with rather than aids the dyeing process.

Although empty peanut-butter jars work just fine for mixing dyes, I recommend a half-liter wide-mouthed jar. It will hold approximately two and one-half cups of mixed water and dye and is deep enough to easily keep three eggs at once covered with dye, shallow enough to assure the eggs a safe landing. The wide mouth allows you to easily lower eggs in with a spoon. Finally, a rubber ring keeps the closed jar airtight for storage, so the dye lasts longer.

NICE-TO-HAVE EXTRAS

The eggs, kistkas, beeswax, and dyes you choose need to meet specific requirements to help make sure you produce beautiful pysanky. But the tools and supplies in this section are more a matter of your own preferences and needs—you can more easily "make do" in this arena.

Stainless-Steel Spoons

You'll need to buy or accumulate stainless-steel spoons that you'll use only for dyeing eggs—thrift stores and garage sales are good sources. I've found several soup-spoon size slotted spoons, which have the added convenience of allowing excess dye to drip back into the jar. (I leave the spoons in the dyes during my work session, then rinse and dry them when I've finished for the day.)

Wax-Heating Materials

To keep the wax liquefied in a nonelectric kistka, you need candles and household matches. Household candles, or candelabra candles after they have burned down to six or eight inches, work well. A simple, low candle holder is perfect. (Votive candles or candles in jars are less satisfactory, as their flames are less exposed.) You can also use a lighted candle for removing wax from the egg in a later stage of the process.

Paper Towels and Facial Tissues

You need paper towels for patting the egg dry when it is removed from the dye bath. I use the same towel through one complete egg. Because most eggs are dyed in a progression from lighter to darker colors, the dye accumulating on the towel will not discolor the egg. (When the dye sequence changes, which you'll read about in chapter 4, it is important to be aware of dry dye on the paper towel.) Although any brand is fine, I recommend the most absorbent, and I prefer plain white.

Facial tissues are ideal for the wax-removal stage of the decorating process. The plain white, cheaper brands work well—avoid those with softeners.

Drying Board

When using the oven (anything from toaster oven to full size, but not a microwave), either for removing the wax from the eggs or for drying them out, you'll find a homemade or purchased drying board very convenient. Ready-made versions have nails hammered through one side of a wooden board, forming triangles of points on the opposite side upon which the eggs can sit to heat. Before I acquired one of these, I stuck three thumbtacks per egg through a piece of cardboard and set it on a cookie tray, which worked fine. My favorite drying board is one I concocted from four rod stilts designed for use in potters' kilns. I can fit six or eight of these on a cookie tray. The advantage to this method, particularly in the final coating stage, is that the stilts entirely support the egg from the inside—nothing touches the egg's surface. You may end up using both kinds of drying boards, when you have many eggs in a variety of stages.

Remember to remove the drying board from the oven (and to use it only for wax melting and egg drying). Your wooden board won't burn up during the melting and drying processes, because the temperature is set so low.

But on occasion I have accidentally left a drying rack in my oven and preheated the oven for baking, until someone says, "Does anyone smell something burning?"

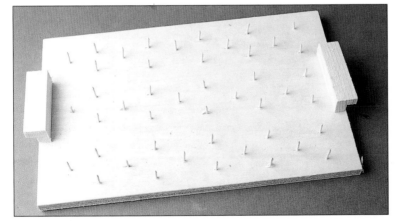

Drying boards will prove so handy you'll probably want to either buy one or make your own. This wooden board is one ready-made style available.

Remove the wax from eggs by heating them in an oven on a drying board made with rod stilts.

Egg Blower and High-Speed Tool

For years I blew out the inside of my eggs with my bare lips. Anyone who has used this method learns that it is difficult, risks breakage, and often leaves one's cheeks in questionable shape. Of the several suitable egg blowers on the market, I prefer the Blas-fix, which requires making only one hole in the egg. It includes a tool for making the hole as well as a simple pump with a long hollow tube that allows you to pierce the yolk and blow out the insides.

Like an egg blower, a high-speed (30,000 rpm) hand tool is optional but enormously helpful. Created for hobbyists, it has different bits that perform all kinds of tasks, from drilling holes to sanding. I use it to cut eggshells for jewelry and have found it the best tool for drilling holes before removing the insides. (If you're just starting out, I'd advise waiting to buy one—an egg-blower kit tool works fine for making the hole.)

Toothpicks and Needles

Many things can clog a kistka besides the commercially blackened wax mentioned earlier. Tiny pieces of dust collect on the beeswax and end up in the tool, accumulating into small waxy dust balls. You simply need to keep several declogging devices on hand—pointy-ended toothpicks and a variety of beading needles (available at craft stores). Running either of these into the well of the tool and through the point often clears the clog. If the wax still doesn't flow smoothly, try twisting the corner of a facial tissue to a point and cleaning out the well.

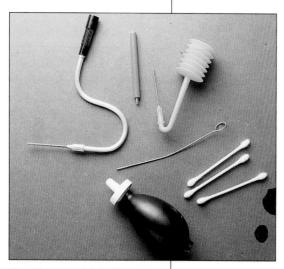

Egg blowers with bulbs attached work by hand, not mouth; the curved-tube type pictured here requires your breath to push the egg out.

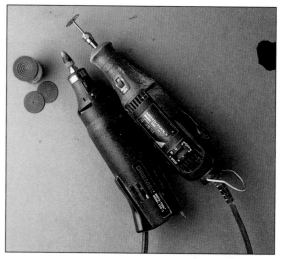

High-speed tools are useful but optional, especially for beginners. Left, a basic model with bit attached for drilling a hole in the egg; right, a deluxe version with variable speeds, with a cutting disk attached. Also shown are extra cutting disks.

Gloves, Knife, Pencils, and Spot Remover

Wearing a disposable latex glove on your egg-holding hand keeps the egg clean and free of fingerprints—especially since your fingers will usually have dye on them. To slice off small pieces of wax, using a small knife saves your fingernails. Use pencils to help map out the divisions of the egg (although for years I refused to), and spot remover to get the last bits of wax not cleaned off by the candle or oven method.

Magnifier

You may find some form of magnification essential (as I now do). Some egg decorators favor the lamp/magnifier combinations, but I use a tool that jewelers and dentists wear on their heads, available in a variety of magnification levels—I choose different-powered lenses depending on the closeness of the work.

Polyurethane and Polymer

One method of adding a gloss finish to completed eggs calls for a high-gloss polyurethane, available in eight-ounce cans at most hardware stores. A second technique uses a two-part polymer coating, available at most full-service hardware stores.

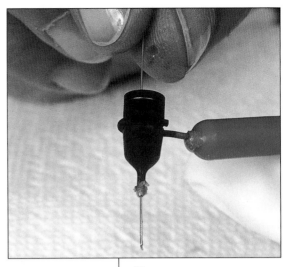

Two ways to remove unwanted clogs from the kistka's point—beading needle and twist of paper towel.

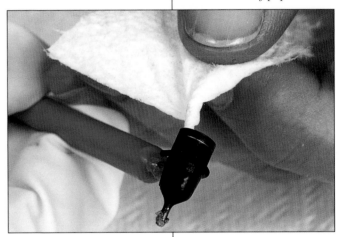

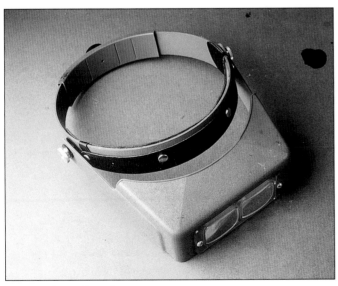

A magnifier such as this one favored by dentists and jewelers often proves helpful with close work.

Chapter Three

Decorating an Egg: From the Beginning

Before you do anything well, you often have to do something first. So it is with egg decorating. I find preparing the materials for the craft with care not only a pleasing process in itself but one that makes the decorating experience far more enjoyable. And the quality of the finished egg depends on how caringly and carefully the preparations have been done.

SETTING THE STAGE

Because a refrigerated egg perspires in your warm hand, an egg must begin at room temperature for decorating. The melted beeswax will not adhere to a moist surface. (One occasionally reads about preparing eggs by placing them in a vinegar and water bath before starting the waxing process. Since it would expose the eggs to a preliminary coating of the mordant that helps set the dye, it probably would be worth trying. I have never used the technique because it's an extra step—I simply take the egg from the carton and begin decorating.)

Besides having the egg at room temperature, taking care of a number of other preliminaries will make the work flow more easily. Have some safe receptacle available to prevent the egg from rolling off your work surface. An empty egg carton makes a perfect resting place for the egg in process if the phone rings or you need to set it down for any other reason. When I first taught this craft in high school, my classroom was furnished with drafting tables set at a forty-five-degree angle. That we had few eggs break was a great tribute to the students' seriousness of purpose.

Many egg decorators like to have a pencil line to follow when they begin waxing their designs onto the eggs. A number-two pencil works fine for drawing the basic divisions of the design lightly on the surface of the egg. (More experienced egg decorators may choose to skip this step.) The advantage to lightly drawing in the pattern is that it eliminates the guesswork when it is time to apply the wax. As you proceed through the dye sequence, the darker dyes cover the pencil lines.

You may prefer to use wide rubber bands to divide the egg. A thin masking tape can serve the purpose as well. You may then outline these marking devices with a pencil, or you can simply draw next to them with the kistka.

While I seldom take the time to do this next preparatory step, I am always pleased with myself when I do. Having a pile of pellet-sized beeswax chunks ready to put into the kistka is like finding your car's gas tank unexpectedly full—it's one less thing you have to do in the midst of trying to get somewhere. You can shave pieces of beeswax from the cake with a small knife, then roll them in your fingers into a shape that easily fits the kistka's well.

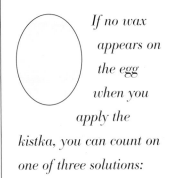

If no wax appears on the egg when you apply the kistka, you can count on one of three solutions:

- *Heat the kistka more thoroughly.*
- *Unclog the kistka.*
- *Be sure you're holding the kistka at a perpendicular angle to the egg.*

If you have ever dyed eggs, you may have been dismayed by those parallel lines that seem to appear from nowhere when an egg is first dyed. These are roller marks created when the egg was commercially processed, rolling its way down conveyor belts where it was sprayed and washed. The marks won't show up as strongly on every egg, but I have often experienced the disappointment of spending hours waxing on the white shell only to place it in dye and see these markings develop like photographic images in a developer. When this happens to you, take heart. The darkest-color dyes may eventually cover these lines.

(An assistant once helped me by creating snakelike pieces from the blackened beeswax, which I then cut into pellets for loading my electric kistka. This, of course, is something you could do yourself, if—like most of us—you don't happen to have an assistant.)

With precut pieces of beeswax, filling the well of your kistka is simple. Just put one or two pellets into the opening. The best way to heat the kistka is to hold its tip in or next to the top of a candle flame, where the tool will heat most quickly and melt the wax. The carbon from the flame will eventually blacken the tool and wax, which will make the wax lines you draw more visible. As the tool heats and the wax turns to liquid, you can add more pellets to fill the well. You want the tool to be as full as possible without overflowing. The fuller the well, the longer you can draw on the egg before having to refill. But beware—an overly full kistka may drip unpredictably onto the egg and interfere with your design.

Before I begin to draw on the egg, I always test my kistka on a piece of paper to make sure the wax is flowing smoothly. To test your kistka, take a few short strokes on the paper. The line should flow smoothly and be of the same width as the diameter of the kistka tip. If the line comes out runny and thick, the tool may be too hot. If the line is scratchy or won't flow smoothly, the tool may not be hot enough or it may be slightly clogged.

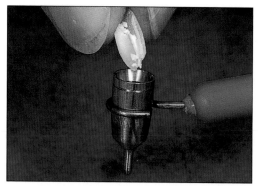

First steps include filling the kistka's well with pellets of beeswax.

A key to applying wax evenly is to keep the tip of the kistka perpendicular to the egg surface.

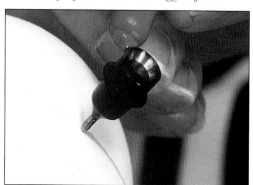

Holding the kistka's stylus slightly above the flame heats it more rapidly.

DYEING AN EGG

Together we will work through a very simple step-by-step egg-decorating and dyeing process that I have seen decorators of all experience levels use successfully. At your worktable you have room-temperature white eggs in an egg carton or nestlike holder. Your wax is chipped into small pieces, ready to be inserted into your kistka. For this egg you will use the traditional colors of Ukrainian Easter eggs—yellow, green, orange, red, and black. (After your first creation, I think you'll feel more confident about experimenting on other eggs using the different color sequences we'll explore later in the book.)

Mix the aniline dyes in your glass jars according to the directions on the packet. With your dyes mixed and your egg at room temperature, you now fill, heat, and test your kistka before proceeding to step 1.

Step 1

On the white egg, outline a pattern lightly in pencil if you wish, or draw directly with wax from your heated kistka—all of the wax lines will remain white on your egg. *The most important thing to remember when applying the wax to the egg is that the tip of the tool must be perpendicular to the surface of the egg.* The wax is drawn onto the shell by capillary attraction (the "pull" between a liquid and a solid that are touching—remember from high-school science?). Holding the tool at even a slight angle to the egg lessens the effectiveness of this natural attraction. When you turn the egg, always keep the tip of the tool in direct contact so that the wax can be pulled out of the kistka onto the eggshell. For me, one of the most pleasing parts of the process is applying wax onto the eggshell. The smell of the beeswax and the smoothly flowing lines have an elemental and sensuous quality that makes the craft the simple pleasure that it is.

Choose any geometric or abstract shape and draw it over and over on the entire egg, with each repeated shape having some contact with those around it. (If you have drawn your lines in pencil, now go over them with wax from your heated kistka.)

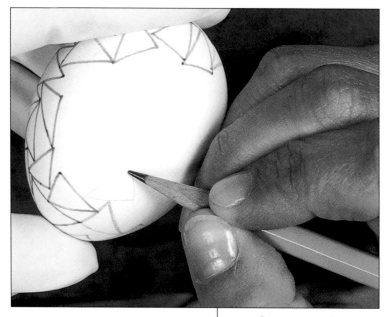

Draw connecting geometric shapes with pencil, then cover the lines with wax from the kistka...or draw the shapes freehand directly with the kistka.

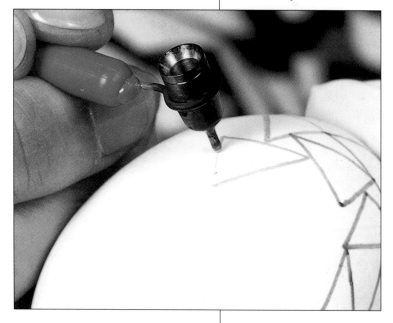

31

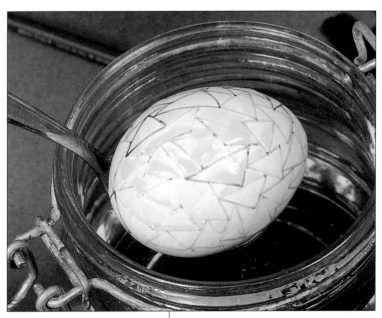

Gently place your egg on a large spoon and lower it slowly into the jar of yellow dye until the spoon touches the bottom. Allow the egg to roll off the spoon into the liquid. Because these aniline dyes are so fast acting, lift the egg out after a few seconds to see if the color has reached the intensity you want. If it hasn't, lower the egg into the dye for a few more seconds. When the color looks right to you, spoon the egg out of the jar. Lift the egg off the spoon with a paper towel and pat it dry. Keep the towel for subsequent dye baths, but keep it far away from your candle flame. Once you have dried the egg off, you can immediately begin the next step.

When you remove the egg from the yellow dye, lifting the egg off the spoon with a paper towel allows excess dye to drip back into the jar—saves on dye and paper towels both.

Step 2 *(on the yellow egg)*

To get a small amount of green (a "cool" color) into this combination of basically "warm" colors, you may now apply dabs of aquamarine dye by hand rather than dipping the whole egg into the aquamarine dye. Use a toothpick (or a small paintbrush), which will allow you to target a small dab of dye exactly where you want it. For this design, dab a dot of aquamarine into the center of each of your shapes. Be careful as you turn the egg that the area you just dabbed is dry. Otherwise, your fingers may smudge dye onto areas of the shell where you don't want it. When you have dabbed aquamarine into each shape and the dye has dried, dot on wax from the kistka to cover each dot. The dots will now remain green, and future dye baths will not be affected.

Aquamarine dye dotted onto the yellow shell produces small green accents.

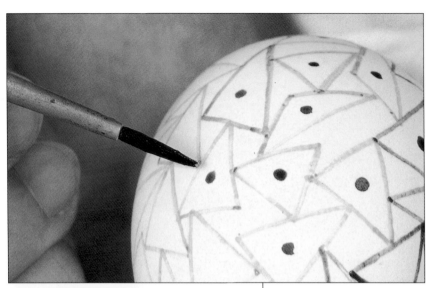

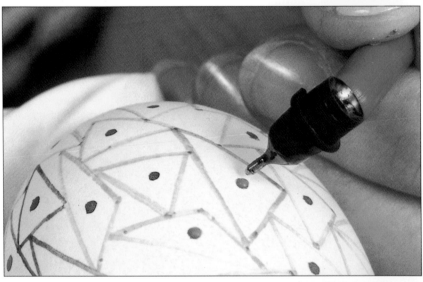

These two processes—protecting the green accent dots with wax...and waxing in the inner geometric shapes to keep them yellow—can be accomplished in one step when you feel more confident.

Step 3 (on the yellow egg with green dots)

Now it is time to put wax on the shell in the areas you want to remain yellow. With the kitska, create a simple shape around each green dot inside each of the larger shapes. You can choose to repeat the shape of the outside design or draw something completely different, but each inner shape should be the same. It should not fill the whole area inside your original shape, because you need to leave room to add more colors. Once you have drawn around all the green dots with wax, dip the egg into the orange dye, using the same technique as in step 1.

When you remove the egg from the orange dye, you will be able to see four colors on your egg—the white outlines, the green dots, the smaller yellow shapes surrounding the dots, and a background of orange.

With the egg removed from the orange dye, draw in the lines you want to remain orange—four colors will then show under the wax: white, yellow, green, and orange.

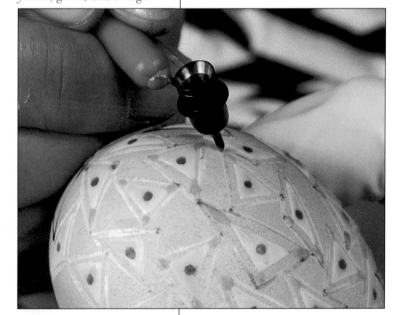

Step 4 *(on the orange egg)*

Using any kind of lines you like, with wax from the kistka connect each small yellow shape with the large white shape that surrounds it. (These lines will remain orange.) Dye the egg red.

Step 5 *(on the red egg)*

To give your design a red background, fill in all of the background areas between the shapes with wax. (The only unwaxed surface remaining is the area between the orange geometric shapes and the white outlines.) Place the egg in the final dye bath, the black. Sometimes the egg needs to sit longer in the darker colors in order to achieve complete saturation and to cover the lighter colors. Although your egg may have lots of dark wax on it, you will still be able to see the colors underneath just waiting to be revealed.

When the egg comes out of the red dye, you cover all areas outside the geometric shapes with wax—only small areas will remain to receive the final black dye bath. (The black in the photo is blackened wax.)

35

REMOVING THE WAX

Two methods use heat to remove the wax from the egg. One is to hold the egg to the side of the candle flame. I call this the instant-gratification method because you can watch the colors reveal themselves as the wax melts, a process I never fail to find exciting and rewarding—it's like unwrapping a present. Hold the egg in the lowest part of the flame and to the side of the wick to prevent the carbon from blackening the artwork. As the wax begins to turn to liquid, wipe it gently with an absorbent facial tissue, then put it back near the heat.

While melting the wax off with a candle is truly gratifying, it has obvious risks. Holding the egg too long in the heat can cause gasses to build up inside the shell—the egg may burst. Another hazard of using this method is that the carbon that was helpful in blackening the wax in your tool can now leave an unsightly dark stain on your egg. Holding the egg very low in the flame should prevent this disappointing result. Dewaxing an entire egg in the heat of a candle also requires more patience and reserve than I can usually claim. Sometimes I like to use this method only long enough to get just a peek at what the colors will look like, then set the egg aside to go with the other finished eggs into the oven—the second method for dewaxing eggs with heat.

An oven is excellent for removing the wax from several eggs at one time and poses no threat of carbon staining. I recommend setting your waxed eggs on the drying rack. Rather than trying to transfer a loaded rack into the oven, put the empty rack in the oven first and then arrange the eggs on the nails. Close the oven door and set the heat at between 225° and 250°F (107° and 121°C), depending on your oven. It is always better to heat the eggs longer at a lower temperature than to risk damage from overheating.

The wax should become liquid enough to remove after twenty or thirty minutes. Be sure to have a safe place ready for the finished eggs, such as an empty egg carton. Leave the drying rack in the oven. Lift an egg out with the tissue, wipe it off, and then go back for the next one, leaving the oven on throughout the process. Because the egg will begin to cool as soon as you take it out of the oven, sometimes you need to put it back in to reheat to complete the process.

While I don't use chemical substances to remove the wax from my eggs, turpentine or lighter fluid are adequate to the task. If you choose this method, you'll need to wear protective gloves and to work either in a well-ventilated room or outdoors. Pour the liquid onto a piece of cloth and gently rub it over the waxy surface until it comes clean. I do use a chemical solvent as a final cleaning agent for any wax left after dewaxing with heat. A paper towel is sufficient for this process, but again I caution you to use protective plastic gloves and ventilation.

After the egg has been emptied and the wax removed by candle or oven heating, it needs to be oven dried to bake any remaining contents onto the inside of the shell. In my early years of egg decorating, I did not make this a practice. I thought the eggs would naturally dry out, but occasionally I would find a yellow puddle under an egg I had decorated and stored. I now routinely oven dry every egg for one hour on the drying board with the nails. To do this, place the eggs on the board with the hole facing up, so the contents will not drip out and cause a problem around the hole. Set the oven temperature to warm, and bake the hollow, decorated egg for one hour.

An aluminum-head kistka works well for applying extra protective wax to the area where the hole will be made.

Two ways to make the hole: a manual drill or an electric drill.

BLOWING THE EGG

For thousands of years, makers of pysanky allowed their eggs to dry out naturally over a period of time. The albumin, the egg white, evaporates through the porous shell. The yolk dries out and either rattles around inside or adheres to the inside of the shell, causing a Mexican jumping-bean effect—the egg always rolls to the heavier side.

A perfect tool-drilled hole.

At just what stage of the egg-decorating process to blow the egg is a matter of choice. Some practitioners work on blown eggs from the start, which to my mind presents more problems than it solves. You would need to cover the ends of the egg to prevent dye from flowing in. If you wax the ends, those areas will never receive the dye—the egg will be white on the ends. Also, the empty egg will float on the dye, so it would need to be weighted to submerge. If you do not wax the ends and allow the dye to flow into the shell at each successive dyeing, you face a long wait between dye periods while the inside thoroughly dries out.

I recommend blowing the egg after it has gone through all of the dye baths. Although the obvious risk then lies in breaking the egg after you have decorated it, if you are careful this happens very rarely. A less obvious risk of working with fully dyed eggs is that egg white will discolor them. One way to avoid this possibility is by removing the wax, varnishing the egg, and letting it dry on the nail drying board before removing the insides. Inevitably, when I have used this method, small flecks of dried polyurethane adhere to the nails, leaving tiny areas of shell unprotected.

I prefer another technique for preventing discoloration: Before you remove the wax from the egg, add wax to the area where you will be making the hole, covering any exposed areas that might be sprayed accidentally when you blow the contents out. Apply this wax the same way you apply wax to large areas. You needn't be terribly cautious here. There are no lines to stay within, just shell to protect. Once the area is covered, you can safely create the hole.

The egg's contents exit through the same hole the egg-blower is inserted through. It's essential to pierce the yolk with the needlelike tube, so it can flow out.

For years I suffered sore cheek muscles and strained lips from blowing the egg liquid out through a pinhole, using my own air power, but I have finally found a small hand pump that has made egg blowing quite satisfying. Although the many egg-blowing kits include an adequate device for making a hole, I favor drilling the hole with an electric rotary power tool (as described in chapter 2.) If you try this, hold the egg firmly in one hand and allow the tool to do the work. Hold the bit next to the waxed end of the egg and let it make the opening. With either method, you need only one hole.

If you're not blowing the egg out by mouth, follow the directions of the egg-blowing device you have chosen. One type offers a small hand pump with a long hollow needle that you insert into the hole and push up and down to pierce the yolk. (The major cause for breakage in blowing eggs is a whole yolk trying to fit through a tiny hole.) When you see yellow on the needle, you know that you can begin the process of blowing air inside. Gently squeeze the pump and allow the air pressure to push the insides through the hole and out of the egg until the egg feels completely empty. You can then pour water into the pump and repeat the process to cleanse the inside of the shell.

With the egg now dyed, waxed, and blown, it is time for the removal of the wax, a process often called the miracle of the eggs and by far my favorite part.

The miracle step—melting off the wax. To prevent carbon blackening, hold the egg low and close to the flame and absorb the melted wax with a tissue.

For easy dewaxing, poke three thumbtacks through a piece of cardboard to support the egg and heat the wax off in a toaster oven—no carbon blackening to worry about.

FINISHING THE EGG

A simple and good way to finish your decorated egg is to coat it with a high-gloss or matte-finish polyurethane. Make sure to use a product that is *not water soluble*; anything else could smear your entire design. Some products that are not polyurethanes also give a shiny finish. *Be sure to select a polyurethane.*

Wearing disposable plastic gloves, dip the fingers of one hand into the can of polyurethane and dab some of it into the palm of the other hand. Now, pick up your egg and roll it around in your palm to coat the entire surface evenly with polyurethane, using your fingers and the rolling motion of the egg to help the process.

This is where the rod-stilt drying board comes in the handiest. Place the coated egg onto one of the stilts and allow it to air dry for at least eight hours—or whatever time the directions on the polyurethane label recommend for best results. The stilt drier is excellent because no area of shell is resting on anything.

A second and far more complex method for coating the eggs involves using a two-part polymer resin. Polymer resins must be mixed according to very specific instructions, combining a resin and a hardener in premeasured amounts, either by weight or by volume, depending on the brand. As an example of how the process compares to coating the eggs with polyurethane, here's how to use one two-part polymer resin. To coat one egg requires a teaspoon each of resin and hardener. Measure these with a plastic spoon, wiping it off thoroughly between pourings. Mix the two in a small disposable clear plastic cup. Stir vigorously for two minutes with a wooden stirrer—the blended liquid will appear thick and bubbly. Pour it into a small, shallow box, like a jewelry box. Wearing gloves, roll the egg in the resin mixture until it is completely and evenly coated. Place the coated egg on a thin dowel stuck into a piece of polystyrene plastic or some comparable set-up. This will allow any excess resin to drip down. After fifteen minutes wipe off any drips that have formed with a disposable foam brush. Wait another fifteen minutes and again wipe off any accumulated drips. After a total of forty-five minutes has elapsed, the resin will have gelled enough that no further drips will appear. Cover the egg set-up completely with an empty cardboard carton to keep it dust free. Within twelve hours the egg will be dry to the touch. It is best to wait twenty-four to seventy-two hours before setting it into an egg carton or wrapping anything around it.

DISPLAYING THE EGG

How to display your miniature masterpieces? Gift shops and stores that sell Ukrainian Easter egg supplies offer many models of egg stands. But you may want to seize this opportunity to stretch your creativity even further, for many objects can serve as imaginative pedestals or nests. A few I have used or seen cradling pysanky:

- candle holders
- napkin rings
- French egg stands
- egg slicers
- real or commercially made nests
- baskets
- small grapevine wreaths with moss in the center

And can you imagine any centerpiece more beautiful than a bowl filled with dozens of your glowing eggs?

Disposable gloves protect your skin from the polyurethane that will give your egg a high-gloss finish and provide a smooth surface for coating it.

A cardboard and thumbtack do-it-yourself drying stand gives the coated egg total exposure to the air.

Chapter Four

Playing with Color

When I first saw a carton of pysanky, I found the beauty of the colors enchanting. I loved their depth and brightness and what seemed to me their vast number. What I have realized over the years is that the intricacy of the patterns and the beauty of the craft create the illusion of many more colors than actually appear on the surface of the eggshell. Also, most decorated eggs are displayed in groups, which exaggerates the multicolored effect. A traditional Ukrainian Easter egg has at most six colors, including the white of the shell itself. The traditional palette contains only white, yellow, green (just a touch), orange, red (sometimes a light red and a darker brick red), and black.

Red, yellow, and blue are the primary colors from which all other colors can be mixed. You mix red and yellow, for instance, to make orange. These three colors—red, yellow, and orange, the colors of sun and fire—are known as *warm* colors or a warm range; they make up a color *family*. When blue is mixed with red to make purple, or mixed with yellow to make green, the results are known as *cool* colors or the cool family or range— purple, green, and blue, the colors of water, grass, leaves, and so on. When you're working with eggs and dyes, the colors actually go on top of each other, and usually the darker colors will cover the lighter—orange will cover yellow, red will cover orange. If you've ever mixed paints, you know that when you mix colors from different families—say, orange and blue—the result is an unattractive muddy color. If you place an orange egg in blue dye, the same thing is likely to happen—mud.

Warm colors—red, oranges, yellows—seemed perfect for these Peruvian cat eggs, inspired by pre-Columbian tapestry and pottery.

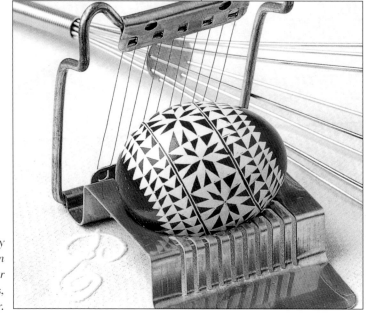

One color used at full intensity has its own drama—here on an egg inspired by the Lemoyne star popular among quilt makers, displayed in an egg slicer.

The colors red, yellow, orange, green, blue, and violet are also called *hues*. If you're mixing paint, all colors can be made from these. To create paler versions of the hues, known as *tints*—pink, light yellow, light green, and so on—you add white paint. Since there is no such thing as white dye, to create tints for dyeing eggs you add water to dilute the intensity of the hue. The more water you add, the lighter the color. Adding increasing amounts of water to pure red dye, for instance, will create lighter and lighter tints of coral.

The intensity of color on an egg also varies according to the length of time the egg sits in a dye bath. The longer you leave the egg in any dye—whether a full-strength dye or a tint—the stronger the color will become. If you place a white egg into a dye jar for five seconds, it will emerge paler than an egg you leave in the same dye for five minutes.

The dye sequence traditionally follows a simple progression from the lightest color (yellow) to the darker colors (orange, red, and black). Green, representing a different family of colors, is applied in dabs on designated areas once the shell has been dyed yellow, then promptly covered with wax to seal the green color. The process then continues—the yellow areas are covered with wax, the egg is then dyed orange, and so on (see pages 32–35).

A good way to approach the process of creating tints is to use a pure dye (say, pink) plus two watered-down versions—one with just a couple of tablespoons of pure dye in the water (making pale pink, in this example) and one about one-half dye and one-half water (making rose, in this case). Experiment with varying combinations of dye amounts and dyeing times. Soon you will feel comfortable with the way that works best for you to achieve a range of tints based on one color.

Once you are an old hand at dyeing eggs in variations on just one color, try combining tints of two colors on one egg. With only two colors of dye and their tints you can give the egg a multicolored look because of the range of shades possible.

Two intensities of aquamarine enhance this double-wedding ring design.

Three variations on one color: Adding two tablespoons of full-intensity aquamarine dye to a cup of water produces a tint of aquamarine. To deepen the color, dip the egg in the same diluted dye for a longer time. Finally, use full-strength dye for the true color.

A Double Rainbow: Combining Color Ranges

After you have done a dozen or so eggs in the standard light-to-dark sequence, adding dabs of green for contrast, you will probably be anxious to get more variety in your palette. If you are worried that after you put in a lot of time on your wax design it will be ruined by an unattractive color, take a dozen or so white eggs—no waxing—and just experiment with the dyes—see what happens as the egg passes from one color to another. This playing with color is something many kids do instinctively, but adults—especially adults who know the color "rules"—may hesitate. I encourage you to simply plunge in.

As you become intrigued by color and design, you'll probably discover, as I did, that your fascination with egg decorating increases dramatically when you understand how to work with both color ranges on the same egg—that is, how to combine the oranges and reds with the blues and greens without ending up with mud. It is possible to accomplish this. Variations in color are achieved not by mixing the dyes with each other but by using different dye sequences.

These paisley eggs combine tints of red and pink dyes that range from the lightest pink wash to fuchsia and carmine.

Two points should help you understand the process of working with two color ranges. First, aniline dye colors do not combine on the egg in the ways you were taught on the color wheel in art class. Mixing yellow and red does not always make orange, mixing yellow and blue does not always make green, and so on. Learning how the dyes work and how to manipulate them is exciting, challenging...and frustrating. Second, you may put two eggs through the same sequence of dyes and end up with matching eggs, or you may end up with eggs that look different from each other. The dyeing process is affected by the freshness of the eggs, the exact length of time they sit in the dye, the humidity, the temperature, and the receptivity quality of each eggshell. The rule of thumb is, It all depends.

You'll find you can work elaborate designs by varying the intensity of just one dye color.

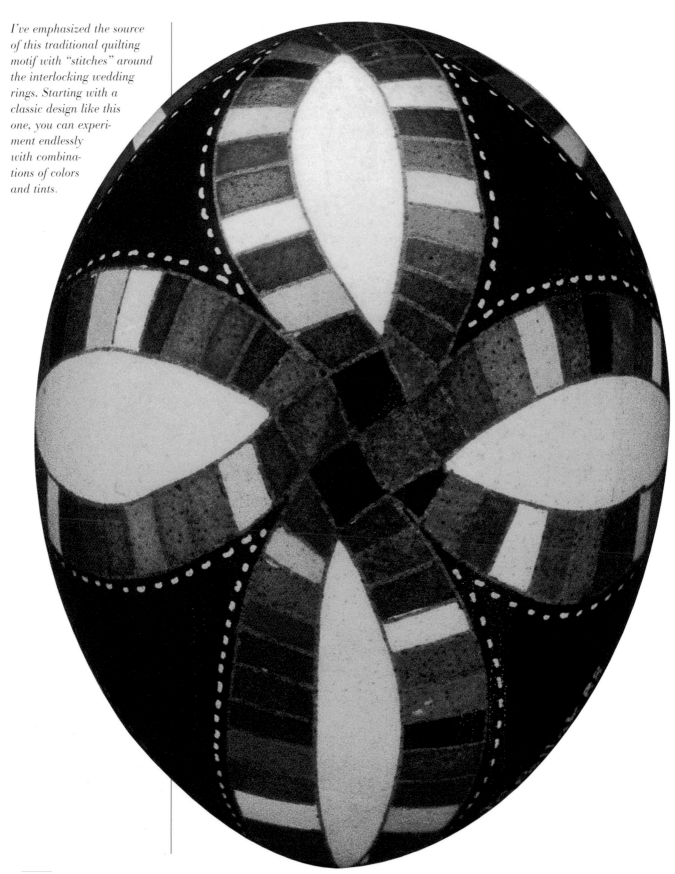

I've emphasized the source of this traditional quilting motif with "stitches" around the interlocking wedding rings. Starting with a classic design like this one, you can experiment endlessly with combinations of colors and tints.

There are two ways to move from one color palette to another, from warm colors to cool ones (for instance, from red to green), or vice versa. The simpler method requires using a bleach solution; the more intriguing method involves learning more about how aniline dyes work.

USING BLEACH TO CLEAR YOUR PALETTE

Think of bleach as an eraser. Whatever color your egg is dyed, dipping it into a bleach solution will erase any color not covered with wax, returning the shell to its original color (white or brown). You can actually see the color lifting off into the bleach bath.

Let's say you want to create a stained-glass look on your egg, and you need to have black outlines to give the effect of leading. Dye your white egg black and draw these outlines with wax (see chapter 5 on two-color eggs for more about drawing on the black egg). Now place the black egg with the wax lines on it into the bleach solution. The black lines, protected by wax, will stay black. The black dye on the rest of the shell will bleach out to the shell color—white or brown. If you then dye the egg red, all but the black outlines will become red. You then cover the areas you want to stay red and place the egg back in the bleach to prepare for the next color. When it comes out of the solution, it will be red in the areas covered by wax, with black lines. Now you might put the egg into the green dye—you'll have a black, red, and green egg. You continue bleaching and applying wax until you have all the color areas you want.

Soon after I discovered this process, I began decorating most of my eggs by placing them first into brown dye, then drawing the wax outlines, rather than doing the outlining first as I recommend in the basic steps in chapter 3. When the egg is then dipped in the bleach solution, bleaching out all the color except the dark dividing lines under the wax, those lines look gold against the bleached white background. Then the normal dyeing process can begin.

Dark outlines on decorated eggs give the design a different feel than the traditional white outlines found in pysanky, and simply changing the color of the outline can change the entire feel of the egg. For instance, a black outline can create the look of stained glass, while a red outline lends an Eastern quality to the design.

While I have read of restrictions that should be followed when using bleach, such as a twenty- or thirty-minute drying period between bleaching and succeeding dye baths, I have ignored such rules with no unhappy results. One cautionary word about using bleach: It removes some of the natural dyeing properties from the eggshell. This means that certain colors are difficult to use after the egg has been bleached, particularly yellow and orange. In my experience, these colors never reach the intensity you see in yellows and oranges dyed before bleaching. One solution is to figure out where in the design the yellow and orange areas will be and dye and wax those areas first. The difficulty here is in knowing exactly where those areas will be without the benefit of the outlines. A way to work around this challenge is to substitute brown for yellow. Brown absorbs nicely into the shell after bleaching, when it turns a golden color. You can then turn it reddish orange by placing the egg briefly in the scarlet dye.

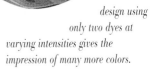

An all-over design using only two dyes at varying intensities gives the impression of many more colors.

45

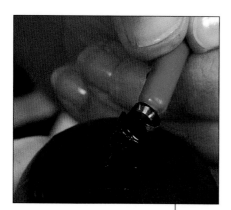

How it works: Creating the stained-glass look—black outlines—begins with dyeing the egg black, then applying wax (here, in an X-shape simply to show the process). Next, bleach out the black dye outside the waxed X (the reddish color in the solution is actually black dye lifting off). You can then go on to add other colors.

For a striking black-on-white egg, you can wax all of the areas that will remain white (the darkened wax areas in the photos), then dye the egg black.

For these Lemoyne-star earrings, I waxed the white areas and dyed the eggshell black.

I created the gold lines in these quilt-inspired eggs by dyeing the eggs brown, waxing, and bleaching. Besides brown, white, and black, the Lemoyne-star design has only two additional colors; the classic American schoolhouse design has four.

EXPECT SURPRISES

Apart from using bleach, the other way to move from one color family to another is by taking advantage of the most intriguing factor about the aniline dyes: You can't expect the traditional results when you mix colors; instead, you can expect surprises.

Chart eggs: If you're intrigued by color, you may want to spend time experimenting and documenting dye sequences and your resulting color discoveries.

To illustrate what can happen when you try different color sequences, I have created dye charts on several dozen eggs using the colors brown, yellow, orange, scarlet, pink, aquamarine, light blue, violet, and purple. As you can see in the photos, hundreds of colors can be created with only nine basic colors. You can also see how fascinating these dyes can be and

More chart eggs: For my own records, I note the original color, how long the egg sits in each subsequent color, and the order of the dye baths.

The rub-off effect that first struck me as a mistake I later came to see as a way to create texture and interest on an egg, a look that resembles acid-washed fabric.

The effect of color is apparent in these three eggs, all with the same design. The traditional Ukrainian Easter-egg palette of the black egg conveys a different feeling than either the red-outlined Chinese look of the red egg or the black-outlined stained-glass colors of the purple egg.

what fun you can have playing around with them in various combinations. Most of the chart eggs show the initial dye color, followed by a second color, and then the result of placing the egg back in the first dye bath.

The possibilities of trying different dye sequences are nearly endless. For instance:

You can achieve the same color in more than one way. Different shades of green can be created through several combinations—some of these you might have predicted (light blue or aquamarine over yellow), some may surprise you (yellow over purple). To create green, dye an egg

- light blue over brown
- aquamarine over brown
- aquamarine over light blue
- brown over aquamarine
- yellow over purple
- light blue or aquamarine over yellow
- aquamarine over orange

Certain color combinations will cause a rub-off effect, which can be desirable or upsetting depending upon the design. This often happens if an egg is left in purple dye for longer than ten minutes, for instance. The effect can be used to your advantage—it creates a denim or acid-wash look.

An egg placed in one color, then dyed a second color, may yield a third color when placed back in the first color (pink - aquamarine - pink/purple).

An egg placed in one color, then dyed a second color, may revert back to the first color when placed back in the original dye (yellow - pink - yellow).

Reversing the order of two dye baths may create a different color than that produced by the original order. A pink egg placed in aquamarine dye will yield different results than an aquamarine egg placed in pink dye.

How long an egg stays in a dye bath significantly affects that dye color and all the colors that come after it. You can create a great variety of colors simply by changing the length of time the egg spends in the dye. (Other factors affecting coloration are the age of the egg, the age of the dye, humidity, and room temperature.)

Repeating the same dye sequences may yield different results (lighter, stronger, more of one color).

As you experiment with dyes, you'll gather a lot of information about how various individual colors act in combination. I've learned, for example, that:

Yellow is a good base color for any other color. That is, light blue, purple, orange, red (scarlet), pink, and aquamarine all show up as their true hue when dyed over a yellow egg. Yellow also changes some colors (pink, for example) back to yellow. Yellow dye on a purple egg gives the purple a lighter, greenish effect.

Orange is unstable. It causes a mottled effect in some dye sequences (orange - purple - orange). An orange egg dyed yellow becomes completely yellow. Orange followed by light blue creates a streaked or mottled texture on the egg.

Brown dye as a base coat will transform subsequent dyes to warm versions of their hues. For instance, an egg dipped into brown and then into red will take on a richer, deeper red hue than an egg dipped into yellow, then red, or an egg simply dyed red.

Aquamarine and **light blue** can be used almost interchangeably. When used as the first color in a sequence, they yield very close results after each subsequent dye bath. I prefer aquamarine because of its intensity and rapid dyeing power, but light blue can be effective in a different way.

Pink has several unusual properties. A pink egg placed in aquamarine dye will turn a beautiful blue. Placed back into pink dye it turns fuchsia—intense pink. Back into the aquamarine and it becomes a deeper, richer blue. The same two dyes—pink and aquamarine—yield different results when the order is changed: Place an aquamarine egg into pink dye and it will turn periwinkle—a purplish blue. A pink egg left in yellow dye for three minutes will turn yellow. Left in orange dye for three minutes, a pink egg becomes orange.

Red followed by three seconds of aquamarine turns a purple-brown that I don't find particularly pleasing. If you leave that same red egg in the dye for about three minutes, it turns a rich deep blue green. Red followed by yellow sometimes creates a mottled red under a yellow egg. Red followed by orange will become orange.

Purple as the first dye bath yields darker color variations. A purple egg placed in orange results in a mottled brown-orange. Placed back into purple, it turns a deep rich purple. Placed again into the orange, it turns a lighter tint of the first brownish orange.

You're probably beginning to see that you have thousands of possible color combinations to choose from by playing with color sequencing, tints, and timing—and that luck plays a role too. You can achieve almost any color. Still, even though an almost infinite number of colors may be attainable, too many colors in a design are not desirable. Remember how colorful only six colors seemed on an egg's very small surface.

Sometimes the container can be the inspiration for color or design.

Chapter Five

Easy Does It: Simple Two-Color Designs

One way to become more comfortable with the wax-resist process is to spend some time creating designs in wax without concerning yourself with all the color possibilities. The result of this wax doodling can be a very beautiful collection of two-color eggs. You can work on the white egg or dye it a solid color and then begin applying wax. After you have covered as much of the surface as you like (in this case, more is better), dip the egg into another color and remove the wax. You've just made a two-color egg. This is especially fun and useful if you want to try out different texture effects, like cross-hatching or pointillism (the small dots used to fill in an area that you see in Impressionist paintings). Try working with kistkas of different sizes to experiment with how the thicker and thinner lines look in a design. There are no rules.

In many two-color designs, one of the colors is the undyed white eggshell, and one of the most effective two-color eggs is the black-and-white combination. With a strong design, you can make even a simple checkerboard or triangle pattern very powerful, as you can see in the Mexican-stamp design eggs on page 59. In the most intriguing designs, it is difficult to determine what is foreground and what is background. The eye is captivated by the push and pull—it wants to keep looking, to figure it out, to understand the relationships of shapes to spaces. (If you're familiar with the work of M.C. Escher, your own eye has probably been fascinated by the push and pull of his use of shape and space.) Achieving this play on the surface of the egg is challenging and rewarding. When it works— when you remove the wax and the two-color combination sings—here is no greater joy.

Just for fun, doodle on a plain white egg with your kistka, covering most of the surface with wax designs.

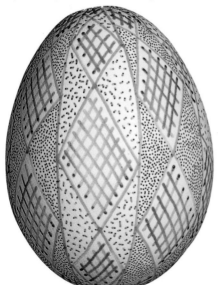

For contrast, dye the egg a strong color—red, dark blue, or black.

Melt the wax off and amaze yourself with what you've created.

What first led me to try two-color designs was the search for something a little bit easier than the time-consuming, labor-intensive process of making intricately patterned and multicolored pysanky—even though I loved the work. Surely I could find ways to eliminate steps or in some other way simplify the process. For me, as you will see as this chapter progresses, trying to make things simpler does not always produce that result. Two-color eggs turned out to be slightly less time-consuming (at first), because they require only one dye bath—two if the base color is something other than white. But for an interesting result, the egg still needs to be well covered with wax, which is the labor-intensive aspect of the craft. And the waxing for two-color eggs seems to take longer. (It's all done at once, at the beginning, rather than in stages as in the multicolored eggs.)

Limiting yourself to two colors gives your creativity plenty of room to roam. The simplest experiment is to reverse the colors. For an interesting pairing, try the black-white combination on two eggs—use black as background on one and white on the second, as in the photo of eggs and fabric on page 91.

To see how greatly color influences design, use the same design on two eggs. First do it in black and white. Then do it again in, say, yellow and red, or light aquamarine and darker aquamarine. Most people like to display eggs in groupings. Staying with one design and varying the two colors on each egg, you can fill a very large bowl—a gorgeous visual display of variations on a theme.

To go a step further, break the solid areas into textured areas, but keep to your range of two colors, as in the three photos of the red-and-white egg on page 53. In these textured areas you can use dots, cross-hatching, stripes, a checkerboard, or any other repetitive design you like. You can also use tints and shades of each of the two colors (see chapter 4).

For a two-color egg, first dye the unwaxed egg a solid color. Then either draw your design in pencil and go over it with wax...

Or draw directly with wax. Creating a surface that is about equal parts waxed and unwaxed will produce an intriguing positive-negative effect.

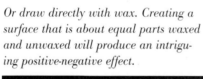

Leave the egg in the second dye bath long enough for the color to reach full intensity. The play of the two colors—the way they advance and recede to the eye—gives this design visual depth and interest.

Using the two-color process requires trust and persistence, because along the way you cannot tell how your design is working. Not until you have applied all of the wax, dyed the egg the second color, and removed the wax is your design clearly revealed. Sometimes I scratch off some of the wax ahead of time just to see how the combination has worked. For me, waiting is the hardest part of the process. (The accompanying series of photographs follows an egg through the two-color sequence, using red and yellow.)

SNOWFLAKE DESIGNS

Besides looking for an easier, faster process when I decided to try two-color eggs, I also wanted to give the egg a function beyond simple display. What I came up with was a holiday ornament—on the front was an intricate white snowflake pattern on a red ground, on the back I wrote "Christmas" and the year.

Simplicity itself, one might think. Just one dye bath. But I couldn't leave well enough alone. I found that the red became richer if it was achieved through a series of dyes—yellow-orange-pink-red. (The same base of colors is required for a purple or aquamarine background—that is, yellow-orange-pink-purple or yellow-orange-pink-aquamarine; for a rich green, dye the egg yellow or brown and then aquamarine.) The underneath colors gave the final color a depth that I couldn't achieve with soaking the egg in that color alone. And, I have come to believe, the extra work is always worth the effort.

Two-color snowflake eggs make cherished Christmas gifts as well as unusual tree or table decorations.

To make your snowflake egg a hanging decoration, cut a length of ribbon or thread to more than twice the final hanging length you want. (Here I've used three-ply gold lamé thread.) Holding the two ends together, tie a simple knot. Clip off the extra tails.

Pierce the center of the knot with a straight pin, and slide the knot to the middle of the pin.

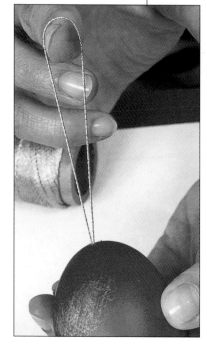

Slide the entire pin—knot and all—into the hole in the top of the egg. Pull gently on the loop to position the pin and knot inside.

If the snowflake pattern appeals to you, you'll find inspiration for designs everywhere, once you start looking. All you need is one elaborately drawn arm—repeated five more times. I find doodling a convenient way to come up with new ideas. As a reference and starting point, you may want to refer to a volume of photographs of thousands of snowflakes and snow crystals. For me, books on lace designs, paisley patterns, art nouveau, and art deco have all served to inspire new snowflake patterns.

When you are ready to draw your snowflake on an egg, you want the design to be centered. To establish center points on two sides of the egg, you can draw a pencil line around the vertical and horizontal axes of the egg. Use one as the middle of the snowflake and the other to provide a line for the message on the reverse side, if you choose to add one—if you don't want to include a message, you may want to make a simplified snowflake on the back.

In the eggs pictured here, you can see a variety of ways for creating the six-sided center you need for your snowflake. The principal ones I have used are a hexagonal, six dots, interlocking triangles (Star of David), a circle with six points located on it, and—the trickiest—intersecting lines at sixty-degree angles. Once you've established the center, continue the design by repeat-

To make a bow, wind the thread around three fingers several times and tie it in the center with another piece of thread.

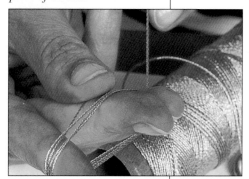

With a dab of hot glue from a glue gun, hide the hole and stick on the bow.

An heirloom—your finished holiday tree or wreath ornament.

ing lines or shapes and rotating the egg. (Draw the entire design lightly in pencil before using your kistka, if you choose to—you may want to review the steps in chapter 3). The process can be very rhythmic, meditative, and enjoyable. The design builds and builds until you have a beautiful, symmetrical composition. On the back, write your message in wax.

If you want deep, rich color, take the time to place the egg for a minute or two in succeedingly darker colors, starting with the lightest in the range (for red eggs: yellow-orange-pink-red; for green eggs, yellow or brown, then aquamarine). After the egg is dyed to the desired color, remove the wax.

If you intend to use your egg as a hanging ornament, the hole for removing the contents needs to be drilled at the top (if you didn't include a message on the back, you don't need to worry about which is the top). Empty, dry, and coat the egg according to the steps in chapter 3.

Snowflake eggs make delightful and unusual holiday decorations, whether you hang them on a tree or wreath, from a mantel, or in a window or arrange them festively in a bowl or nest.

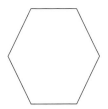

Hexagonal template

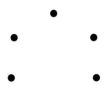

Six dots freehand

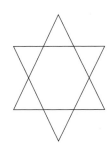

Interlocking triangles

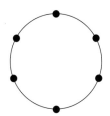

Circle with six points

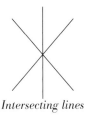

Intersecting lines

One arm of snowflake pattern

Repeated five more times

LACE DESIGNS

Sometimes you'll find that a source you're exploring for one kind of design inspires an entirely new creative train of thought. When I was searching lace references for two-color snowflake patterns, I selected a few lace patterns that interested me in the way they used shape and space. While this is not a beginner's project, if you enjoy close, concentrated work (like counted cross-stitch), it is achievable.

For the lace eggs, draw a series of closely spaced parallel lines at ninety-degree angles to form a very fine graph or grid pattern. Then lay out the lace design by applying wax to the inside of each square, as in the pattern I've reproduced on the eggs pictured here.

I worked these lace designs on white eggs, then dyed them a single color. Design ideas are everywhere—I adapted the bird pattern for the red egg from this book of lace designs.

MEXICAN-STAMP AND JAPANESE-STENCIL DESIGNS

Even if you don't consider yourself an artist, once you've begun decorating eggs, you'll probably begin searching out inspiration for new designs. What I look for are strong, graphic images, particularly ones whose use of shape and space I find fascinating. Two sources I have found especially rich in motifs are Mexican- stamp designs and Japanese-stencil patterns. (If you are a beginner, I suggest you try these designs later in your egg-decorating career—in spite of the simplicity of the motifs, the process is not easy.)

These Mexican-stamp motifs are deceptively simple—the black-and-white designs present a special challenge, even for more experienced egg decorators.

Found in Mexico and in parts of the United States, ancient Mexican stamps were originally used in the decoration of clothing, pottery, and paper. First made by hand from clay, they were later formed from molds. The oldest and most common motifs are geometric designs based on circles, squares, and triangles, as well as variations on these themes—spirals, stair steps, and zigzags. Plant and animal designs followed, and eventually the two patterns were combined .

The Japanese-stencil designs use familiar, purely Japanese motifs from nature and work, often combining the two. A popular design, for instance, was called irises and nail pullers. Cooking pots and weaving patterns were often juxtaposed with cherry blossoms or open fans. Kimonos served as the primary canvasses for these artistic expressions, which were created during the Edo period, an era of peace and artistic freedom that lasted from the early seventeenth until the middle of the nineteenth century.

I made two of these Japanese-stencil eggs by working on the white shell, and one I dyed black first.

For the Mexican series I chose primarily red, black, white, yellow, and orange, with some other colors for additional interest and variation. On some of the eggs I applied the wax to the undyed shell; on others I dyed the egg black, coated it with wax in the designated areas, and then bleached it to remove the dye outside the waxed areas and allow the white shell to be seen there. It is easier to draw the black areas than it is to draw the spaces around them—thus my decision to dye the egg the darkest shade first. (For instance, if you want to have a large black cross on a white-background egg, it is easier to dye the whole egg black and outline a large cross with wax and fill it in, then bleach the egg back to white—see the photos on page 46.) When someone looking at one of these eggs cannot figure out which area I drew and which serves as background, I feel the designs have succeeded.

Two conditions will make your work on black eggs easier. For me, one absolute necessity is exceptional lighting. I have overhead lights in my studio. Whenever I work on an egg, especially one at a very dark stage, I also use a halogen lamp that shines over my left shoulder (I'm right-handed) directly onto the egg to keep the wax lines visible. In addition to good lighting, use unblackened beeswax—it's more visible on the dark shell.

The reason beginners may find these Mexican and Japanese designs discouraging is that they are tricky to lay out on the egg. They do not come in the conveniently geometric sections of traditional pysanky. The free-form designs (the pots, for example) are simple, but most of the others require a few dividing lines on the egg for placement. Because there are no templates for these unusual shapes, you draw them freehand on the egg's surface, which requires excellent concentration more than artistic flair. No one is requiring you to recreate the shapes—drawing your own interpretation of the design element works equally well.

If not in the earliest stages of your egg decorating, I hope eventually you will find these more challenging two-color designs worth the effort.

Each of these Japanese-stencil designs requires only one waxing step, which covers nearly half the egg's surface—the shapes and spaces are of equal importance visually. Lower left, the pattern of irises and nail pullers succeeds if you can't tell which color came first.

Chapter Six

Going Ethnic: Ukrainian Easter Eggs

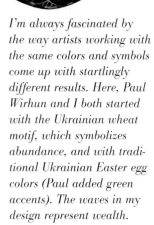

hile every decorated egg has its own beauty, Ukrainian Easter eggs are special. Whenever I have taught classes in pysanky or brought eggs of this design to craft shows, people have been mesmerized not only by the beauty and intricacy of the patterns but by something deeper they perceive in the designs. They are right. Each Ukrainian Easter egg tells its own story. Most begin with a promise for everlasting life in the form of an eternity band that encircles the egg. Others promise fertility, success, or long life.

One customer came back to my booth a year after purchasing one of these eggs to tell me how much it had meant to her. I asked her what design it carried. "It had a stalk of wheat on it," she said.

"Did you have a bountiful year?" I asked.

She looked startled. "That's exactly how I would describe this past year."

I told her that the wheat symbol promises the recipient a bountiful harvest. It is often surrounded by a wave pattern that represents wealth. The wave symbolizes water, which Ukraine—the breadbasket of Europe—depends on for its crops.

I'm always fascinated by the way artists working with the same colors and symbols come up with startlingly different results. Here, Paul Wirhun and I both started with the Ukrainian wheat motif, which symbolizes abundance, and with traditional Ukrainian Easter egg colors (Paul added green accents). The waves in my design represent wealth.

UKRAINIAN LEGEND AND TRADITION

Each Ukrainian Easter egg is designed with symbols and colors intended to bring the person who receives it love, health, fertility, or whatever attribute the artist selects. Pysanky have always been powerful talismans—bringers of good fortune.

The word *pysanky* derives from the Ukrainian root word *pysaty*, meaning "to write." Pysanky are also called message eggs—literally, eggs that have been written on. One Ukrainian legend claims that the fate of the world depends upon the making of pysanky. A chained monster of evil sends out messengers every year to see how many pysanky are being made. If the report comes back that few have been created, the chains of evil are loosened and evil flows throughout the world. But if the messengers say that pysanky are being made in great numbers, the chains are tightened and evil is restrained. Perhaps when you take up your kistka, you will find it a comforting or inspiring thought that you are helping keep the chained monster at bay.

In Ukraine, for ages before the birth of Christ and continuing after the Ukrainians adopted Christianity in A.D. 988, these intricate masterpieces were decorated and exchanged in the spring. As in so many cultures, the egg as a life symbol was thought to possess extraordinary powers for healing and good luck. Recipients of the decorated eggs were assured of good health, wealth, good fortune, protection from the elements, success with their crops, good friendships, and esteem.

Many legends surround these beautifully colored eggs. The Virgin Mary is said to have carried eggs to the soldiers at the foot of the cross. As she pleaded with them for mercy for her son, her falling tears left brilliant dots of color on the white eggs. Today, Mary's tears remain one of the ideas symbolized by colored dots on the eggs. (Part of the legend tells us that when Mary knelt to pray for Jesus, the eggs rolled out of her apron and were distributed throughout the world—giving birth to the tradition of Easter-egg rolling.)

Making pysanky became a Lenten ritual in Ukraine. A typical family produced—or wrote—about sixty eggs for Easter Sunday, distributing a few to the priest, placing one or two into the feed troughs of the farm animals and in the beehives to insure abundance and honey production, and leaving three or four on family graves. A dozen or more went to children and godchildren, and about the same number to the young girls of the family to present to certain young men as signs of affection. Some were held back for the very ill, to place in their coffins, and several were kept in the home for protection.

Daniel Saracynski adapted pysanky technique and intricacy to his own designs, like this geometric wonder bright with dots, the traditional Ukrainian symbol for the sun, stars, or Mary's tears.

The intricate eternity bands on these three eggs by Daniel Saracynski incorporate some traditional Ukrainian symbols—colored dots (Mary's tears), stars (God's light and love), and crosses (rebirth, life).

It was the responsibility of the women in a household to make all these special eggs sometime during Lent. Designs and color recipes were closely guarded secrets, handed down from mother to daughter. Making pysanky was not a social event but an elevated ritual performed in near silence and privacy at the end of a day sanctified by refraining from gossip, argument, or sin. A wholesome meal would have been eaten, and the youngest children would be asleep. Only then would the women utter the prayer "God help me" as they began their work. They also prayed that the receiver of the eggs would be endowed with joy, good fortune, happiness, and protection from harm.

THE SYMBOLISM OF THE IMAGES...

The women created each egg with a message or symbol tailored to its intended recipient. Giving it was an act of friendship, an expression of fondness, and in some cases an offering of forgiveness for wrongs done throughout the previous year.

Young children received the most brightly colored egg designs, the elderly the darkest. Gray was used for departed souls. A young married woman with no offspring might receive an egg with a chicken on it to help her fertility. If that did not work, the next year her husband might receive one decorated with a rooster on it, or later still an oak leaf to promote his manliness. Married couples often received forty-triangles designs, signifying not only the forty tasks in life (such as the birth of children, health of the master, strength, and so on) but the three primary elements of fire, air, and water or the three wonders of the sun, moon, and stars—and later, the three persons of the Holy Trinity. Farmers received eggs decorated with wheat patterns and wave patterns, promising bounteous crops and wealth.

The *egg* itself represents life; it embodies the eternal cycle of creation.

GEOMETRIC SYMBOLS—circles, triangles, and so on—are the oldest designs and form the foundation for many other symbols (the circle for the sun, for instance).

Circles symbolize protection—evil cannot penetrate them—as well as everlasting life, continuity, and completeness. The circle also represents the sun, the center of the universe, and cycles of life.

Triangles stand for the elements of air, fire, and water, for the Holy Trinity, and for the sun, moon, and stars. *Forty triangles* can stand for the forty days of Lent, for Christ's fast, or for the forty life tasks of married couples.

Suns symbolize the life-giving, all-embracing, all-renewing nature of God (and in pagan times the sun itself was worshiped as a god). A sun also represents fire and warmth, enchantment, prosperity, and good fortune. The most ancient and significant symbol, the sun appears on almost every egg as a small circle or simply a dot.

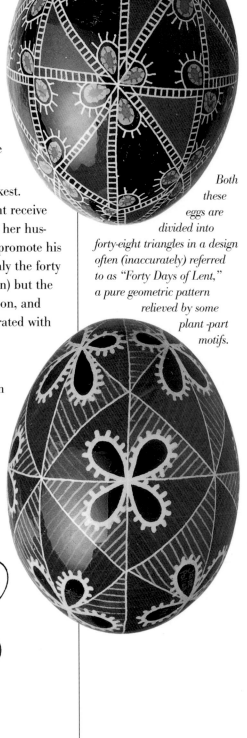

Both these eggs are divided into forty-eight triangles in a design often (inaccurately) referred to as "Forty Days of Lent," a pure geometric pattern relieved by some plant-part motifs.

suns

spirals

Churches dominate this four-part egg, divided lengthwise, with the sieve pattern and triangles as secondary symbols.

Leaves, flowers, stars, and suns create a theme for this eight-part design.

Tripods represents man, woman, and child or birth, life, and death.

Stars and *roses*, both highly popular symbols, stand for purity, life, the giver of light, or the eye or divine will of God, and God's love for humanity. They may also represent success, knowledge, beauty, elegance, and perfection.

Dots usually mean stars or the tears of Mary and also can represent the sun.

Curls are symbols for protection.

Spirals represent the mystery of life and death, as well as divinity and immortality.

The *cross* symbolizes life, the four cardinal points of reality, the four ages of man, or the four directions. It may represent rebirth and eternal life, and it may be a symbol of the Crucifixion.

CHURCHES rendered in stylized form were found on eggs in the western Ukraine; a sieve motif inside symbolized the church's ability to separate good from evil.

AGRICULTURAL symbols are popular on traditional pysanky, for Ukraine as an agricultural society drew many of its positive images from field and farm.

Sieves represent the separating of good from evil.

Nets and *baskets* symbolize the containing of knowledge as well as motherhood and the giving of life and gifts.

Ladders represent searching, rising above the petty, or ascending to heaven.

Combs are symbols of putting things in order.

Rakes symbolize a successful harvest.

PLANT symbols, which stand for rebirth and nature, continue to be popular in pysanky, both for their beauty and for their rich imagery.

Trees stand for strength, renewal, creation, organic unity, growth, and eternal life.

Leaves represent immortality, eternal or pure love, strength, and persistence.

Flowers are symbols of beauty, children, the female principles of wisdom and elegance.

Fruit symbolizes continuity, good fellowship, strong and loyal love, and love of God.

Sunflowers represent motherhood, life, or the love of God.

Wheat symbolizes a bountiful harvest.

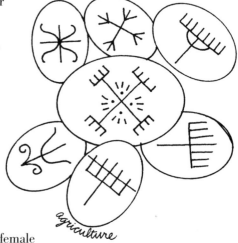

plants

The fanciful bird stylistically
presented on this egg
promises fulfillment of
wishes as well as fertility or
the warding off of evil.

This multidivision egg design
allows a variety of motifs to
be included—here, fish symbols, spirals, comb patterns,
and horns.

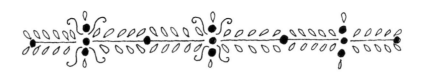

Floral and butterfly designs dominate this two-part egg; you can just glimpse the rich eternity band of flowers and sieve patterns.

ETERNITY BANDS and other dividing elements on pysanky are usually composed of *meanders*, *waves*, *lines*, or *ribbons*, or a combination of these.

Meanders symbolize harmony, motion, infinity, and immortality.

Waves stand for wealth, for it was rain that ensured good crops.

Lines and *ribbons* represent the thread of life or eternity.

Oak leaves, meanders, and spirals dominate this egg divided into quadrants around the middle and wheel patterns on the ends.

ANIMAL symbols offer a wonderful range of messages.

Stags represent leadership, victory, joy, and masculinity.

Horses mean wealth, prosperity, endurance, and speed and may also represent the motion of the sun.

Rams are symbols of leadership, strength, dignity, and perseverance. *Ram's horns* symbolize strong leadership, perseverance, and dignity.

Horns of any kind stand for nobility, wisdom, and triumph over problems. They imply manhood and leadership.

Bear paws represent a guardian spirit as well as bravery, wisdom, strength, and endurance; they also may symbolize the coming of spring.

Birds of all kinds are messengers of the sun and heaven, and represent the pushing away of evil; they symbolize fertility, the fulfillment of wishes, and a good harvest. *Bird parts* (eyes, feet, beaks, combs, feathers) carry the same meaning as entire birds.

Roosters are symbols of good fortune, masculinity, or the coming of the dawn.

Hens represent fertility. Hen feet offer protection for the young and guidance.

Goose feet are symbols of soul or spirit.

Butterflies symbolize the ascent of the soul, as well as the pleasure and frivolity of childhood.

Spiders stand for patience, artistry, and industry, as well as for healing and good fortune

Fish represent abundance, as well as Christian interpretations of baptism, sacrifice, the powers of regeneration, and Christ himself.

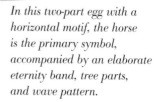

A motif called fish scales divides this egg unconventionally; traditional colors and symbols include triangles, ladder patterns, and horns.

In this two-part egg with a horizontal motif, the horse is the primary symbol, accompanied by an elaborate eternity band, tree parts, and wave pattern.

69

Eight-part eggs traditionally have windmill or three-wing motifs, here represented as wheat sheafs and spirals.

THE SYMBOLISM OF COLORS...

In addition to the symbolism of the drawings on pysanky, each color carried its own meaning. The oldest eggs that have been found were simply two colors. Eggs decorated with four or more colors were considered magical.

White, the egg's own color, represents purity, birth, virginity, and ignorance. A young child, regarded as a tabula rasa, received eggs with lots of white areas.

Yellow symbolizes youth, light, purity, happiness, and wisdom.

Red, the most widely used color, represents passion, love, and enthusiasm.

Orange stands for endurance, strength, and power.

Green is for renewal, freshness, and hope. In Christianity it also symbolizes the victory of life over death.

Brown symbolizes the earth.

Blue represents the sky. Associated also with blue is the good health derived from life-giving air.

Purple signifies patience and trust as well as power.

Black is the color of remembrance, eternity, and constancy as well as of death. The black-and-white combination indicates protection from evil and respect for the dead. Black with red connotes ignorance arising from passion.

With only two divisions and no eternity band, this egg nevertheless creates the impression of having eight parts. Its symbols promise fertility or the warding off of evil as well as wealth and everlasting life.

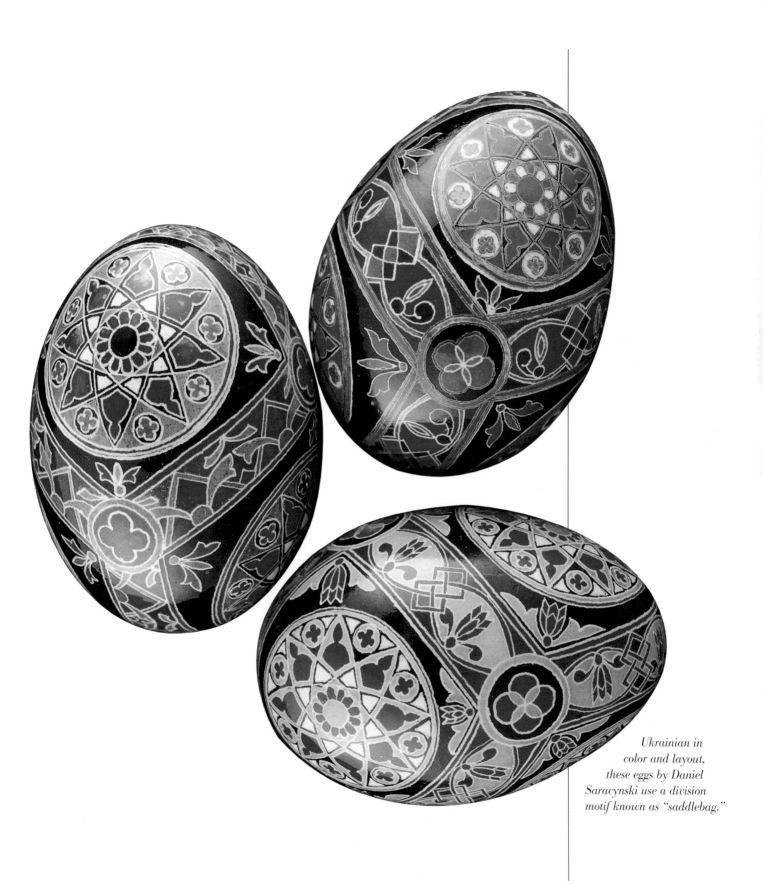

Ukrainian in color and layout, these eggs by Daniel Saracynski use a division motif known as "saddlebag."

Again, an all-over division of squares filled with stars, meanders, basket designs, and ladders.

AND YET MORE SYMBOLISM

Even the beeswax used for writing the eggs has meaning: It signifies the eternal interrelationship of nature and humans. The wax is derived from honey production...honey is collected from flowers...flowers grow in sunlight...some souls become flowers after death...and some souls are born flowers.

The Ukrainians decorated another kind of eggs, krashanky, for Easter rituals. These hard-boiled eggs, dyed solid colors, were used for Easter games and also were placed in the fields to insure good crops and in hazardous locations—such as under thatched roofs to drive away high winds and evil. Their shells were ground up and fed to the chickens to increase their fertility, and young women brightened their cheeks with the red-dyed krashanky, a forerunner of today's blushers.

It was considered a great sin to step on the shell of either a pysanka or krashanka—anyone who did could expect God to punish them with a disease.

The variety of colors and symbols can be combined to create an almost infinite number of exquisite eggs. The only limit is your imagination. Remember that thousands of years of deep reverence and belief in the custom of decorating eggs lend this craft unique power. The eggs you make in the Ukrainian tradition are very special indeed.

Oak leaves, wave patterns, and stars are the major design elements of this pysanka.

An eight-part egg with narrow ribbons dividing the sections; symbols include the star motif, along with triangles, ladders, and dots

A popular way to divide traditional eggs—a broken cylinder around the middle and wheel designs on top and bottom; here the main symbol is the bird, complemented by rakes, triangles, sieves, wave patterns, and suns or dots.

In this more free-form layout, not divided by eternity bands or lines, fish motifs are evenly spaced at intervals around the egg, while pods and sun designs fill in the spaces.

This wide-banded eight-part egg illustrates variations on the flower symbol, including a potted flower, plus triangles or basket designs.

Chapter Seven

Quilting on Eggshells

In the early 1970s I was intrigued by the design of a long wraparound skirt a college friend sometimes wore, made of individual squares of various materials. When I asked where she'd found it, she told me she'd made it. "This fabric is from my bridesmaids' dresses, these are from Chip's old flannel shirts, this square's from an apron of my mother's..." She continued tracing her life history in the cloth. First drawn in by the beauty of the colors and patterns, I felt even more moved by the sentiment behind her creation.

My love affair with patchwork quilts began that day. Far more than utilitarian goods with patterns, they were diaries of women's lives. Not long afterward I saw my first authentic patchwork quilt, and I have been fascinated by the craft ever since.

By a happy coincidence, I learned the basics of Ukrainian Easter-egg decorating at about the same time I learned the beginning how-to's for making a patchwork quilt. That was during the early seventies, with the 1976 Bicentennial Celebration just around the corner, when anything involving U.S. crafts was the focus of a lot of attention and publicity. I began to collect not only any book about quilts I could get my hands on, but also the *Quilters' Engagement Calendar* series, which is still being published today. Here were fifty-two weeks of quilts—large-format, full-color pieces of inspiration. The *Quilters Newsletter*, a monthly periodical, also got my creative juices flowing.

The first egg I designed that combines the checkerboard pattern of quilts with traditional Ukrainian colors and symbols.

Like many other artists and crafts makers, when I come upon a new craft or design that inspires me, I immediately try to figure out how to incorporate it into my own work. I loved quilt patterns, and I loved Ukrainian Easter eggs. But would it be possible to make a marriage? First I designed a Ukrainian quilt, working in many of the traditional patterns, stars, symbols, and eternity-band designs. I even selected colors and fabrics, but I abandoned the idea after completing only two squares in several months (that's about one square a month—it would have been a lifelong project).

As the Ukrainian-quilt idea was percolating, I was drawing what felt like my thousandth Ukrainian star pattern on an egg. It dawned on me that this eight-pointed star was not dissimilar to the Lemoyne star I had seen so often in quilt patterns. What if...? I was enormously pleased with the first egg on which I tried combining a quiltlike feeling with some Ukrainian aspects. Forget the quilt itself—I would figure out a way to put quilt patterns on my eggs.

This stars and hearts design incorporates quilting stitches and some classic Ukrainian symbols and colors.

The shift from Ukrainian to quilt and geometric patterns and colors was complete by the time I designed this asymmetrical star egg.

A nest of quilt-pattern eggs includes some favorite quilting motifs: clockwise from noon, two geometrics, baskets, geometric, tumbling blocks, Lemoyne star, double wedding ring, and Mexican star; inner circle, clockwise from noon, Lemoyne star, geometric, double wedding ring, and red-and-green geometric.

TRADITIONAL PATCHWORK DESIGNS

If you're intrigued by traditional patchwork quilts, you already have your own favorite designs. Mine are the log cabin, the Mexican star, and the double wedding ring. I have tried a variety of layouts of these patterns on the eggs and learned that simply varying the outline color of the quilt design gives the pattern a different feeling.

Probably the most popular quilt design and easily the most widely recognized is the double wedding ring. To start with, you might try simply laying out the double-ring design, choosing various color combinations to fill the bands. Then try experimenting with the way the circles intersect, the variations in background colors, and the different ways the bands can be divided—especially the use of triangles in the bands.

I encourage you to explore all kinds of quilt patterns for inspiration. Another design you may enjoy experimenting with is the tumbling-blocks, or baby-blocks, pattern. It gives the egg a dimension beyond its smooth surface—like Escher eggs, some people suggest. One of the things I enjoy most about the tumbling-blocks design is how the coloring affects how it reads. Even though the grid on each egg is identical, variation comes from whether the boxes are exaggerated or the star designs highlighted.

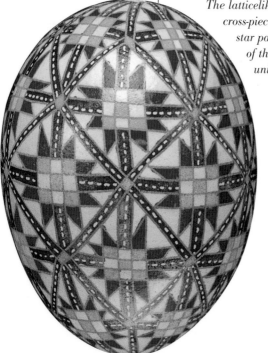

The log-cabin pattern relies on color; here, I've grouped pinks and blues to create the design.

The latticelike effect of the borders and the cross-pieces in the stars of the Mexican-star pattern, along with the extra zip of the applied quilt lines, give it a unique appeal.

An egg with overlapping bands of wedding rings makes an ideal engagement or wedding gift. On this example, the upper band appears translucent, so the lower one seems to show through.

Differences in colors and design size allow nearly infinite variety in double-wedding ring eggs.

Although it appears complex to the eye, the tumbling-blocks layout is actually quite simple, as the line drawings indicate. While you may achieve a meditative state during any wax application, this pattern is particularly conducive to that kind of calm—I find it especially pleasing and rhythmic to execute, with wonderful repetitive easy strokes of the kistka forming diamond after diamond.

Three examples of the tumbling-block design vary only in their colors and their emphasis of different elements of the pattern.

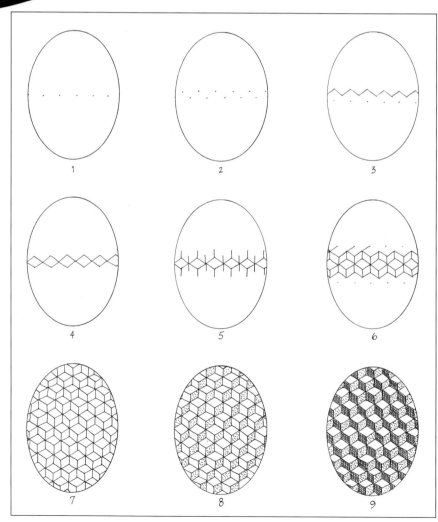

Development of the tumbling-block design.

Similar in structure to the eight-pointed Ukrainian star, the Lemoyne star is another simple and lovely quilt design, whether you choose to work it in two colors or eight. For a change, try using a random-color approach, as shown here, which all but erases the star aspect.

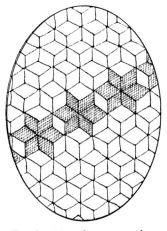

Emphasizing the star on the tumbling-block design.

The Lemoyne-star design looks good whether you use two colors or ten. Left, a random-color approach nearly makes the stars melt into the overall design.

Like me, you may discover that one of the attractions of quilt designs for you lies in their pleasing geometry. I find that the simplest two-color quilt patterns create some of the strongest graphic images. Among these, one of my favorites is the old maid's puzzle, shown here in navy and white with red accents.

The old-maid's puzzle, whose title is traditional if not politically correct, is one of the strongest and simplest of the quilt patterns. I've added red accents to the usual two-color design. Never hesitate to adapt!

I've found the complex basket design, even with its hundreds of tiny triangles to fill in, worth the effort.

APPLIQUÉ DESIGNS

Besides the delightful effects you can achieve with geometric patchwork patterns, another entire area for exploration lies in appliqué designs, including many beautiful floral motifs. Unlike the geometric designs, which are laid out in squares on the egg and are often composed of easy-to-draw straight lines, most of the appliqué patterns require curved lines for vines, buds, and petals. Drawing a curved line on a curved surface is no small feat. I guarantee that with practice it becomes easier and smoother, and the results make it worth the practice. Some of the prettiest eggs you'll make may turn out to be those based on appliqué patterns.

If you're concerned about the amount of background space showing around the central appliqué motif, one solution is to add texture by filling it in with stripes, cross-hatching, or dots—these can be dyed in two tints of the same color (see chapter 5). Filling in is time consuming, but using a medium- or heavy-point kistka makes the task slightly more palatable.

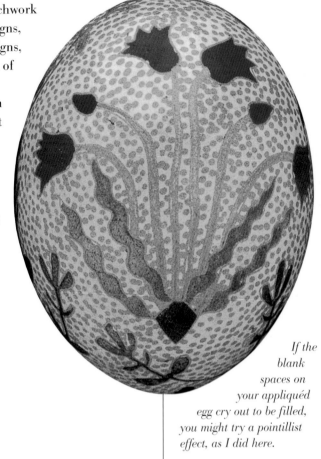

If the blank spaces on your appliquéd egg cry out to be filled, you might try a pointillist effect, as I did here.

Daniel Saracynski created an appliqué effect in this delicate all-over floral design.

You may also enjoy experimenting with some crazy-quilt designs. When I tried them, I got carried away with the stitches, which is exactly what is supposed to happen on a crazy quilt. If what you like about decorating eggs is the rhythm and flow of the design, though, crazy quilts probably won't be for you.

My guess is that we'll never come to the end of quilt patterns as a resource for design. After more than twenty years, I have yet to exhaust the quilt theme as an inspiration in my egg decorating. Exploring the geometry and symmetry of individual patterns, seeing them come to new life on the egg, continues to bring me great joy and delight.

A black-and-white checkerboard offers an arresting counterpoint to the curved lines of this double-wedding ring pattern.

An egg inspired by crazy quilts, which traditionally were made from odd bits of fabric sewn together randomly, then embellished with intricate embroidery.

Chapter Eight

Original Designs Aren't

Where does inspiration come from—for poets, chefs, office workers, gardeners? Where do designers of any kind get their inspiration? Most of you at some time have probably been influenced by an object, color, or style that has "grabbed" you. What will make your egg work unique is the group of stimuli you select to respond to and then reflect in your egg designs.

As most artists learn sooner or later, very little in this visual world is original. What we do with the inspiration when it comes, how it evolves in our minds and hands, is what determines the originality of our work. When you use a source or reference in your work on eggs, you change the medium, the technique, and often the colors. The originality comes from using images usually seen in two dimensions and applying them to a rounded continuous surface. Like the pop artists who copied familiar images (think of Andy Warhol's Campbell Soup can), the canvas has changed and requires the viewer to see the designs in another way. The images you apply to your eggs may often be familiar, but the designs appear new and fresh because they have not been viewed in quite this way before.

TRUSTING YOUR INTUITION

I believe that if you trust your intuition, you will come to know which kinds of images work well for your eggs and which ones do not. My preference is for patterns that are colorful and graphic, often having multiple areas of design. I stay away from abstract, free-flowing images. Whenever I see complex designs composed of subdivided areas I think, "That's for me." In the costume department of the Metropolitan Museum of Art, for instance, at an exhibit that featured party favors from the Napoleonic era, I was drawn to a display of small snuffboxes with micromosaic designs on the lids. Your instincts will lead you in the same ways. Some of us simply have an artistic urge that yearns to divide up space into segments and fill those segments with color.

I find motifs for designing eggs not only when I'm actively looking for inspiration but often when I'm not even trying—from a friend's scarf, the wrapping paper that arrives on a gift, mass-mail catalogues. Walks around your neighborhood may yield a leaf formation or petal arrangement that excites your artistic pulse. Calendars feature artwork weekly or monthly that can serve as a starting point for a design. Keep your eyes open, visit fabric stores and stationery stores, page through museum catalogs. Eventually, everywhere you look, you'll see patterns, motifs, or colors that you want to capture and repeat in your work.

A familiar image made new by Paul Wirhun on an ostrich egg. Paul used a brush-stroke technique to create a textured effect.

Paul Wirhun took advantage of the egg's curve to reflect the gracefulness of tulips. His source was a black-and-white illustration in a book on the structure of wildflowers.

88

A picture file of clipped magazine articles and photographs from catalogs is a handy tool for any artist looking for new ideas. I keep a drawer in my file cabinet for folders with labels such as "Pattern," "Texture," " Palette," "Floral Designs," and so on to jump start my designing mind.

The eggs in this chapter reflect only a small selection of the nearly endless variety of motifs available to inspire us. I've chosen some of the main patterns (other than quilts) that I've found inspiring, along with a sampling of eggs from other egg decorators, to help illustrate the remarkable and exciting possibilities you have to draw from as you explore your own instincts and discover your own sources.

FABRIC AS INSPIRATION

Fabric has proven a rich and inspiring resource for me since the early seventies, when Laura Ashley fabrics were gaining popularity in the United States. Her simply designed cottons often involved only one-color printings of scrolling floral patterns; the white-on-color designs were printed in coordinating colors. In the photograph on page 91, the simplicity of the Laura Ashley design is repeated as it meanders over the surface of the eggshell.

The technique for creating eggs based on fabric swatches is the same as the process for two-color egg designs (see chapter 5), with one addition. You'll be transferring with your hand what your eye sees—that is, rendering the fabric motif onto the egg in a pleasing design that fills the surface. This will be your perception of the motif, your adaptation of it, not necessarily an exact reproduction. Variations on the design are not just acceptable but advisable. When you place your patterned egg in a container with the original fabric piece as a liner or cushion, either an exact replica of the pattern or a loosely structured reproduction will be visually exciting.

While I view paisley patterns as highly interesting (all those compartmentalized areas of color and pattern!), I find them the most difficult to draw on the eggs because of their curving lines and lack of geometry. Where the repeat designs of patchwork patterns offer rhythmic application, the designs for paisleys require intense concentration and attention. Once the patterns have been laid out in the initial wax application, the coloring in of the areas is as straightforward as any other pattern.

Paisleys are everywhere. Fabric swatches available at fabric stores or by mail offer a rich variety of designs, layouts, and colorations. Design books for artists include plentiful references for paisleys as well. Whole books are devoted to them.

My preference is for complex designs divided into sections, like this one inspired by a Persian medallion—the result has the intricacy and feeling of a paisley print.

A greeting card from my files inspired this paisley design.

A pastiche of paisleys—you'll find booksful of paisley patterns, with color combinations (as here) ranging from pastels to jewel tones.

I've found fabric an especially rich source of floral patterns—the first to inspire me were the simple white-on-color designs of Laura Ashley.

Simply designed fabrics with two colors work best. To add interest to a display, try reversing the colors as you move from fabric to egg, as in the black-and-white example here.

CULTURAL DESIGNS AS INSPIRATION

Years ago, Bloomingdale's department store wowed the retail world with an extravagant full-store display theme based on India—shopping bags, aisle decorations, designer showrooms, and merchandise. No store had done anything similar or of such scope. It made the whole visual world open its eyes to other cultural motifs. Moved by a similar fascination, Norwalk, Connecticut, artist Joseph Roll has created eggs influenced by Russian culture—on some of them he includes words from the beautiful Cyrillic alphabet used in Russia. When Paul Wirhun, an artist from Provincetown, Massachusetts, was invited to design a gift for the then head of Russia, Mikhail Gorbachev, he chose a more multinational tack—a globe.

Not just contemporary cultures but ancient peoples fascinate many of us. Many thousands of people thronged to the King Tut exhibit at the Metropolitan Museum of Art in New York City in the 1980s, as you may recall. Among artists of all kinds, the exhibit triggered great interest in ancient designs and colors. If, like me, you're excited by primary colors and two-dimensional qualities, the ancient Egyptian culture is a natural for the kind of designs you'll enjoy creating. Some of Paul Wirhun's eggs reflect his intrigue with Tibetan Buddhist themes, and I've found further inspiration

Russian culture was the basis for Norwalk, Connecticut, artist Joe Roll's design of the czar's crown surrounded by a prayer for God's blessing on the Russian people, a prayer also incorporated into the lyrics of the 1812 Overture.

An egg designed by Paul Wirhun for Mikhail Gorbachev.

Plate V. EGYPTIAN ORNAMENT

On these eggs designed around Egyptian motifs from The Grammar of Ornament, *I thought red outlines would enhance the feeling I was trying to create.*

The Green Tara,
a Tibetan Buddhist figure
that provides salvation for
those in distress, inspired this
ostrich egg by Paul Wirhun.

in pre-Columbian textile designs and have adapted a series of Peruvian motifs on both eggs and eggshell jewelry (see chapter 9).

In the late 1980s and early 1990s attention has turned to the American Southwest and, more specifically, Native American art forms. Artists have tried to capture this spirit on canvas, in photographs, and—in the case of this book—on eggs.

Joe Roll, for example, has designed eggs inspired by images from Mimbres pottery excavated in southwestern New Mexico.

INSPIRATION AS INSPIRATION

Many artists in every medium gather inspiration from the work of other artists, whether in their own field or another. I've mentioned the artistry of M. C. Escher in earlier chapters, and Joe Roll has also found his work a source of inspiration.

Nearly all egg artists, of course, create original designs, and even when we find our inspiration in, for example, nature, our perceptions and style transform the pattern so that it becomes our own unique and individual work.

I found the inspiration for these Southwest-style eggs on a piece of painted pottery (the black-and-white design) and a basket.

Joe Roll drew upon natural images from ancient pottery
unearthed in New Mexico for the birds and animals in these
two eggs (two views of the ostrich egg show a bird on one side,
a rabbit and frog on the other).

Among my own personal inspirations is Daniel Saraczynski, whose eggs appear throughout this book. A surgeon from Bridgeport, Connecticut, who created pysanky as a hobby, he never sold his work. (His widow, Maria, donated their collection to the Ukrainian Seminary in Stamford, Connecticut, which kindly allowed us to photograph it.) Dr. Saraczynski created his own tools from inexpensive ballpoint-pen bodies and hypodermic needles and used electro-cardiogram paper—like very fine graph paper—to divide up his eggs into equal decorating areas. The ultrathin lines and intricacy of his work inspire me with awe, although on a more practical level I was at first most mystified that Dr. Saraczynski's blown eggs have no holes. His secret was to drain the eggs over a twenty-four-hour period using a syringe to remove the insides. He then epoxied pieces of ground-up shell into the hole, so that the egg appeared complete once again.

I have had the opportunity to meet each of the artists who contributed batik eggs to this book. I found that we all share a special feeling about eggs, and each of us greatly admires the others' unique styles and marvels at their discoveries in technique and design. Meetings among egg decorators are rare. I hope the inspiration in these pages will swell our numbers.

Artists inspire artists, as this complicated Joe Roll fish design based on M. C. Escher's work makes apparent.

Artist Dot Discko relies mainly on her own vibrant imagination and years of egg-decorating experience for her glowing designs.

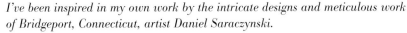

I've been inspired in my own work by the intricate designs and meticulous work of Bridgeport, Connecticut, artist Daniel Saraczynski.

This interpretation of a dunescape is quintessential Paul Wirhun, a Provincetown, Massachusetts, artist— no one else's eye would have perceived the scene quite the same way.

Nature in its endless array of shapes and forms inspires nearly all artists—here, Paul Wirhun recreates dune grass, an image that echoes the traditional Ukrainian wheat pattern.

Chapter Nine

From Eggs to Earrings: Creating Eggshell Jewelry

As lovely as decorated eggs are, there's a limit to the number most people want to display, and after you've decorated your fiftieth or hundredth egg, you may begin thinking—as I did—of how to make the eggs more functional. (Many people are also reluctant to invest in this art form because of the eggs' fragile nature.) What I came up with, eventually, was eggshell jewelry.

The kernel of the idea came from my sister, Meredith, as she listened to the comments of passersby at a craft show. "You know, Jane," she said, "if people could *wear* your eggs, they would buy them." I picked up two decorated eggs and held them under my ears like a funky pair of earrings. We both laughed. But there was a grain of truth in what she said. People admired the designs and colors—they simply did not know what to do with an egg.

The design for this "flying Peruvian" is based on a pre-Columbian textile.

Several years later I enrolled in a course to learn more about developing my business skills and marketing to a larger audience. I learned that I wasn't doing anything wrong—I just had a difficult product to sell. I needed to offer something less fragile and more functional. I thumbed through my library of egg-decorating books for an answer. Table decorations? Napkin rings? No bells went off. Then in Aline Becker's book *Heirloom Eggs* I found photographs of Fabergé-style eggs with doors cut out and hinged open to expose miniature scenes inside the shell. I kept looking at the shape of the doors and thinking that they would make lovely brooches. I knew that egg-decorating catalogs carried precut shells to make this type of eggs. If a catalog company could supply precut shells, I could learn how to cut an eggshell. I read the directions in Becker's book, drove directly to the hardware store to invest in a cutting tool, and began making eggshell jewelry.

EGGS-PERIMENTING

A trial-and-error process accompanies the learning of any new craft or art or skill. I share the stages of my own learning about designing jewelry from eggshells because I'm encouraged when I read about others trying new things (I'm not alone!), because I like success stories, and because my findings may save you some headaches of your own as you begin making jewelry.

Quilt designs, like this flying-geese motif, make attractive earrings...

...and work as well on jewelry as on eggs—here, the log-cabin design.

After figuring out how to cut the designs out of the shell, the big challenge was how to make an eggshell unbreakable enough for jewelry. (Artistry was the least of my worries: I had hundreds of design ideas, and I knew how to work on the surface of the shell.) I spent an afternoon with a friend who makes fine metal jewelry. She and I played with a variety of materials to find out what would adhere to the inside of the eggshell and be attractive and protective at the same time. Epoxy proved the most satisfactory, and for my first jewelry I used a five-minute epoxy available in a dual-barrel dispenser from most hardware stores. It firmed up the eggshell perfectly and conformed to the shape, leaving a level surface on which to attach a jewelry finding, pin back, or earring clip or post.

Since the epoxy was clear, though, it left the back of the eggshell exposed, with all the irregular and unattractive spots left from dyeing. For the first several months I colored the backs of the dyed eggshell pieces, using a gold-paint pen—adding a step to the jewelry-making process. The epoxy was also expensive, which eventually led me to buy gallon containers of shiny black industrial epoxy. This needed to be measured in exact quantities, not by volume but by weight, using a triple-beam scale. Although the results were excellent, I still felt the task of epoxying was taking more time than I cared to spend.

As happens in this universe, taking a creative step outward brings opportunities rushing to meet you. A visitor to my booth at another retail craft show was spending a fair amount of time studying the epoxy backing on the jewelry—unusual behavior. She asked me how I bought and worked with the substance. It turned out that her father had invented a way to package epoxy—the resin and the hardener—in premeasured amounts. She now owns and operates the company her father started. Using her product, I could estimate how much epoxy a batch of jewelry would require, use a 100-gram or 200-gram package, and mix up the exact amount without weighing or measuring—a phenomenal time-saver. I could now create approximately four brooches or four pairs of earrings in the time that it took me to make one decorated egg. Because the jewelry takes up only a fraction of the whole shell, the time I would have spent decorating the remainder of the shell goes to cutting, epoxying, and finishing the jewelry.

"Wearable eggs": The same colors and designs that make exquisite eggs produce lovely brooches.

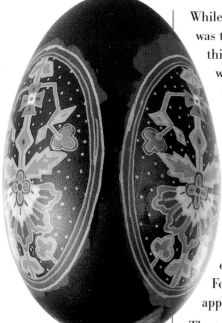

While this time-saving factor weighs less for people who do crafts or art as a hobby (as was true for my friend Daniel Saraczynski, the surgeon I've mentioned several times in this book), those of us for whom crafts are a business are always trying to figure out ways to make more of our product in less time. I have a friend, for instance, who used to create repoussé copper pieces by hammering one piece of copper at a time in a mold. He soon realized that he was not sacrificing quality if he hammered two sheets together into the mold, or even four. I had wondered how I could possibly get four pieces of work with the same amount of effort I put into one. Jewelry making on the eggshells was my answer.

DESIGNING AND CUTTING EGGSHELL JEWELRY

The same designs that make beautiful pysanky will make beautiful jewelry—quilt patterns, Ukrainian motifs, paisleys, and so on. And the same elements that work in egg design work for jewelry as well: a focal point emphasized by decorative motifs. For instance, in the case of jewelry with the Ukrainian wheat design, the same plan applies to the egg and the pin. The individual stalk of wheat is the centerpiece in both.

The tumbling-blocks pattern on the decorative egg is sufficiently interesting to require no other elements. For the pin design, I felt that the all-over pattern should be contained and accentuated with a complementary border, the checkerboard. For another quilt pattern, the Mexican star, I decided minimal bordering was needed on the pin, which closely resembles the layout on the full egg.

Three or four pins— even paisleys, as here—can be drawn on one shell in far less time than it takes to decorate the entire egg surface.

The tumbling-blocks motif transfers beautifully from quilt to egg to brooch. Here, making the brooch from a turkey's speckled eggshell adds interest to the design.

Once you've decided on a design for your jewelry, but before you're ready to begin cutting, you'll need two special pieces of equipment: a rotary hand tool and a cutting box. A high-speed electric rotary hand tool, available at any hardware store or hobby shop, comes with several replaceable heads, each of which performs different tasks. For jewelry making, you'll use the cutting disk and sanding drum head. (Please read the instruction book for a thorough understanding of this tool.) The preferred cutting disk is a diamond disk, which you may need to specially purchase or order, depending on the kit you buy, along with a smaller collet to hold it in place in the tool. The diamond disk makes an exceptionally clean, fine cut and moves through the shell faster than an emery wheel. An emery wheel, though less expensive, will need to be replaced after cutting through about a dozen pieces.

A more major investment and space invader is a cutting box (see photo, page 112), but it's essential for your own protection if you'll be cutting eggs indoors. The egg dust thrown off when the egg is cut is hazardous to your health, so either always do your cutting outside where fresh air will blow away the dust, or invest in a cutting box to vent the dust out of the area you are working in. My cutting box was designed with two armholes for me to reach through, a slanted window to see through and protect my face from the debris, and a bright fluorescent light. I use a vented clothes-dryer hose to blow the dust out the window. Building a cutting box is not a complex construction project; the *Egger's Journal* sometimes carries ads offering them for sale and would be a good source for locating ready-made versions.

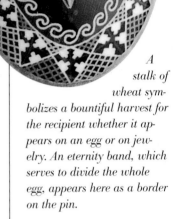

A stalk of wheat symbolizes a bountiful harvest for the recipient whether it appears on an egg or on jewelry. An eternity band, which serves to divide the whole egg, appears here as a border on the pin.

Here, variations in color and detail—such as quilting lines and checkered borders—give the Mexican-star motif a different feel on egg, brooch, and earrings.

JEWELRY ON EGGSHELLS: STEP BY STEP

For creating jewelry pieces from eggshells I recommend using large white duck eggs, which are much larger than hens' eggs and have a thicker shell and a very smooth surface. You can often order these from suppliers with the eggs' insides removed and clean and with holes in both ends. To prepare these eggs for jewelry production, wax over the holes at each end of the egg so that dye will not enter when you dip them in the dye baths.

Note: Although I refer in these steps to making brooches in oval shapes, the technique and steps are exactly the same for making any pins, earrings, or other jewelry pieces. All that changes are the template shape and the layout on the eggshell.

Step 1

Depending on the design of the jewelry, leave the egg white or dye it a light brown in preparation for outlining. (For more details on any of these basic egg-decorating techniques, see chapter 3.)

Step 2

To divide the egg into sections for making oval pins, place a plastic template (available in any art-supply store) with varying size ovals on the side of the egg. It is best to lay the template lengthwise along the egg, because when you cut the egg before filling it with epoxy, this vertical orientation will create the best shape for holding the liquid substance. Choose the oval shape you want, and draw it lightly on the shell in pencil, using the template as a guide. If you wish, lightly pencil sketch in the cross-hairs of the oval to help pinpoint the center of the pin. Sketch the oval two to three times around the shell, depending on the template size and the size of the egg. Don't crowd the ovals—you'll want a comfortable amount of space (about 1/4" or 1 cm) between them when cutting time comes.

Plastic templates are available in a variety of shapes and sizes.

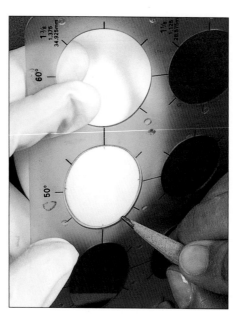

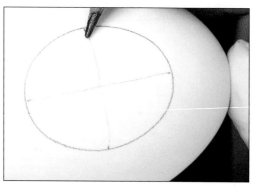

The more flexible the template plastic, the easier it is to work with on the curved shell. (see step 2).

Lines that indicate the center of the oval act as guides for keeping the design symmetrical (see step 2).

Step 3

Use the kistka to draw an outline (over the pencil lines) around the shape of the brooch to indicate the edge to be cut from the shell. You can add an inner border line that will allow you to apply a rim of gold paint to contain the designed area rather than having it reach to the very edge of the finished brooch. Now apply the brooch design as for any pysanky, using pencil then wax or wax alone. Repeat this outlining and design application process for each pin on the egg.

Step 4

Dip the egg in its first dye bath (or bleach). Continue the waxing and dyeing steps, as for any pysanky, until the design is completely rendered in all colors.

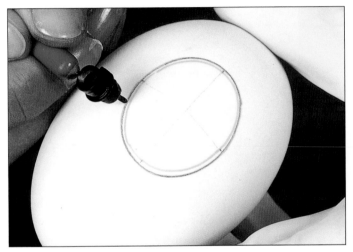

Drawing two parallel lines with wax–a cutting line and an inner-border line–which will later serve as outlines for gilding (see step 3).

As with designs for eggs, jewelry design ideas are everywhere. This brooch has an Egyptian motif ...

...while I based all these pieces on the lotus flower.

Step 5

Remove the wax, as for pysanky. Because these eggs are already hollowed out, the wax-melting process should take only about five minutes, in an oven preheated to 225°F (107°C).

Step 6

When you are ready to begin cutting jewelry pieces from the eggshells, get yourself in position at your cutting box and start up the high-speed rotary tool with a diamond disk in place. Hold the disk a fraction of an inch outside the oval outline to allow for any chipping or splintering—you'll sand this down later. The disk easily slices through the shell, as you follow the outline from beginning to end until the pin shape falls out of the egg. Slowly and carefully,

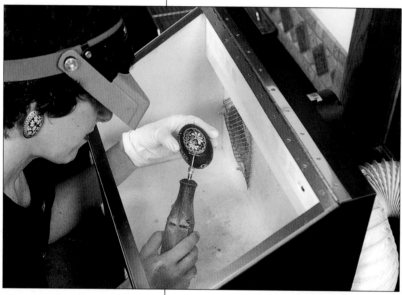

Cutting through the eggshell requires very little pressure— let the tool do the work, as you guide (see step 6).

Cutting slightly away from the line allows for any splintering that may occur (see step 6).

continue the process for the remaining brooches on the egg—extra care is important, because the shell with shapes removed from it becomes increasingly fragile and difficult to hold. Eventually you are left holding a skeleton of an eggshell with holes where brooches used to be. On the floor of the cutting box will be your three or four hollow brooches.

Step 7

Like empty bowls waiting to be filled, place the brooches, concave sides up, on a cookie tray or similar flat container to receive the epoxy filling. Mix the epoxy by whatever method your choice of epoxy dictates—five-minute instant-plunger method or weigh-and-measure industrial process. (When I use the prepackaged epoxy, I mix the contents in the package and then pour the mixture into a plastic squeeze bottle with a Yorker tip.) Squeeze the epoxy into the backs of brooches until each is full to the rim. Unless you have used five-minute epoxy, you now have a twenty-four-hour wait while the epoxy sets.

On these cut pieces and fragments, the splotches on the backs show how dye penetrates the shell (see step 7).

A squeeze bottle with a Yorker tip makes it easy to fill the pin backs with epoxy. A cookie sheet makes a good flat work surface, and spilled epoxy chips right off (see step 7).

Once the epoxy has set (at least twenty-four hours), the edges can be neatly sanded to the cutting line with the cutting wheel with no danger of chipping or breakage (see step 8).

Step 8

Once the epoxy has set, use the cutting wheel (diamond or emery) to sand away the extra fraction of an inch you left in case of splintering during the cutting process, leaving your brooch with a smooth outer edge. To remove extra wax and dust left by the cutting and epoxying, wipe the brooch with a fluid that is 100 percent naphtha, available under various brand names in hardware stores or departments. Wear latex gloves. Paper toweling will hold the liquid and not disintegrate onto the surface as a cotton ball or tissue will.

Step 9

I use pin backs made from nickel. You can attach pin backs to the hardened epoxy surface with any number of adhesives—extra-strength glues and gels and five-minute epoxies. Or

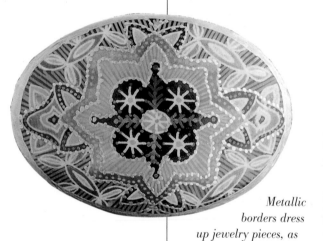

Metallic borders dress up jewelry pieces, as in these paisley brooches and quilt-motif earrings (see step 10). I drew the designs for each brooch from the center medallion of a Persian rug. For the earrings, I tried to give the Old Maid's Puzzle motif a Byzantine interpretation.

another application of the twenty-four-hour epoxy will assure permanent attachment—at the cost of an additional day's wait.

Step 10

To finish your jewelry, you may choose to add a metallic border. Applying this with a paint pen allows you to draw gold or silver onto the eggshell surface more easily than a paintbrush does. Last, apply a coating as for the decorated eggs: polyurethane or the bar-table finish provided by a two-coat polymer. Depending on the coating you select, your brooch will be ready in two or twenty-four hours.

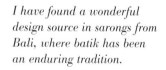

I have found a wonderful design source in sarongs from Bali, where batik has been an enduring tradition.

Ostrich eggs provide the perfect material for barrettes, which need a larger, heavier surface than the duck eggs that work fine for brooches and earrings. For these I borrowed designs from quilts—the double-wedding ring and the flying geese.

111

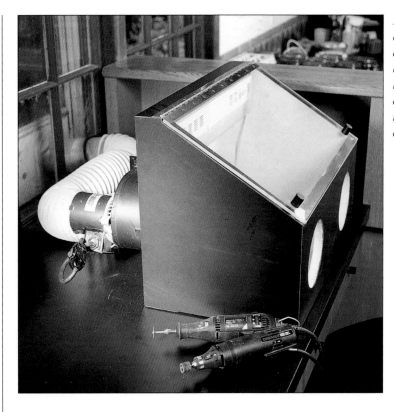

Essentials for making jewelry from eggshells include cutting tools and a cutting box. The box needs armholes, a rigid plastic-covered viewing area, a motor, and a hose to vent eggshell dust outside.

Not only when I'm working in the cutting box but for most phases of egg decorating I've found a kneeling stool takes strain off my lower back.

A Word on Marketing

When I started making jewelry as part of my business, I was all over the map in terms of color, sizes, and designs. In order to bring my wares to the larger audience I was seeking I would need to make some choices. Like many artists, I wanted the world to see all that I had done. But I have found that successful selling is based on selection, which may mean eliminating some favorite designs because they do not fit into any grouping or are too difficult to reproduce. I decided initially to offer designs in four categories, with a selection of pins and earrings in each category. This gave potential customers just a few clear choices—nothing is more frustrating to the artist/seller than having an interested customer who in the end cannot make a decision and chooses not to buy.

Another way to increase sales is to introduce at least one or two new designs or elements at every craft show. Adding earrings, for instance, if you had previously made only pins would be a welcome departure. Adding new patterns to a category—say more quilt designs—would be another draw for the buyer.

One of my greatest thrills is attending a gathering and seeing someone wearing one of my pins or pairs of earrings. The day a photograph appeared on the front page of *USA Today* showing a woman wearing a Japanese tortoise pin I had made gave me real pleasure. Perhaps most satisfying for any of us, though, whether we make this jewelry as a hobby, as a part-time craftsperson, or as a business, are our own jewelry boxes filled with a collection of our designs and artistry.

Many symbols speak across cultures. One customer hoped that wearing this Japanese tortoise pin would remind her to slow down. (This is the same kind of pin that showed up in a news photo in USA Today.*)*

Chapter Ten

Beyond Tradition: Breaking Out of the Shell

Inspiration comes in a variety of guises. For me, it's sometimes an image I see and want to capture. Sometimes it's a color sequence I want to record. And sometimes inspiration is far less romantic. During my egg-decorating career, I had accumulated a half dozen ostrich eggshells that were taking up a lot of room on my shelves. "There must be some way to use these things," I thought one afternoon. (For what artist doesn't want their art out in the world—to be seen, to be appreciated, to be used?) My answer in this case was: ostrich-egg bowls.

OSTRICH-EGG BOWLS

Working on an ostrich egg presents its own set of requirements. Where, for starters, does one get an ostrich egg? While you'll find, once you begin decorating eggs, that lots of people may offer you duck eggs and goose eggs from their farms, no one has yet offered me an ostrich egg. Fortunately, in a small publication called the *Eggers Journal*, advertisers list a wide range of specialty eggs, ostrich among them. They are not inexpensive, running from ten to thirty dollars each.

Laying the wax design onto the ostrich eggshell proceeds as on any other egg. The wax flows on smoothly in spite of the ridges and dimples in the shell's surface.

It may take some convincing before people believe bowls like these are made from ostrich eggs.

The challenge comes when the egg needs to go into the dye. You'll need to make up double or triple batches of dye in a vat large enough for the egg (I recruited a stainless-steel bowl from the kitchen). If you have only one large container, you can pour the dye back into the dye jars and reuse it for each color, with a washing in between uses.

The most efficient way to cut the ostrich egg into a bowl is with an electric rotary hand tool with a diamond disk (see chapter 9). Don't force the disk through the shell; allow the machine to do its job, while you turn the egg as the incision lengthens.

There are two ways to get your ostrich-egg bowl to sit solidly on a flat surface, which you can choose to do either at the beginning or the end of the bowl-making process. The simplest is to provide a stand for it, available through stores and catalogues, which gives it a sturdy three- or four-legged base for the rounded bottom to sit in. The second way is to slightly flatten the bottom of the egg bowl by rubbing it along sandpaper on a flat surface. The shell is thick enough to allow some of the roundness to be sanded away without damage.

Ostrich-egg bowls make surprisingly sturdy containers as well as intriguing decorative accents.

NOVELTY EGGS

I've found that the surprise element is often a factor in the success of designs, even when they're not at all unique. For craft shows, I have used the familiar logos of MasterCard and Visa on my eggs as a signal to passersby that I accept these forms of payment. Although these are widely recognized symbols, people get a kick out of seeing them in batik on eggs.

This experience inspired me to explore other images that might be a surprise for someone to see on an eggshell. In my early egg-decorating days, which coincided with the heyday of the Volkswagen beetle, I made a Volkswagen egg as a thank-you gift for a student-mechanic. He loved it. I challenged my high-school students that year to come up with their own ideas of what would be fun to do on the egg's surface that wasn't Ukrainian. One girl worked with two eggs, creating treads on the bottoms, stripes on the sides, and laces on top to make a pair of Adidas sneakers. Another student created a watermelon, another, a ladybug.

Other ideas evolved when we began to imagine taking the batik technique beyond the traditional. One student created an impressionistic design by filling her kistka to overflowing with the wax, heating it to the point of liquefaction, and then blowing across the top of the tool to spray wet, waxy spots onto the eggshell. She dyed the egg and repeated the process several times, creating a beautiful pointillist effect.

The most familiar of symbols gains new charm (and sometimes humor) recreated on an egg.

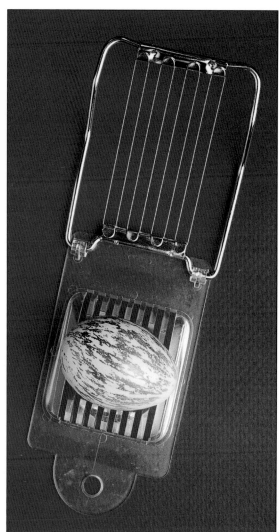

Egg artist Paul Wirhun's watermelon egg on an egg slicer makes an eye-catching display.

117

For a wedding or wedding anniversary, an egg bearing the double-wedding ring pattern makes a distinctive keepsake.

Egg place cards last far longer and prove more memorable than the meal itself—people I know have kept such mementos for decades.

Holidays suggest all kinds of egg possibilities, whether they take advantage of traditional holiday colors or designs associated with the occasion.

When my friend Jon suffered a heart attack, I sent him this egg—red for good luck, and decorated with healing signs and eternity bands.

As I consider all the images I have now seen reproduced on eggs, I believe there are very few that won't work on the eggshell.

Once you begin exploring the possibilities, you'll think of all kinds of new uses for eggs. As place-cards, for example. Since I had neat handwriting, one of my family jobs growing up was to create place cards for the one extended family gathering my parents hosted each year. When I first learned the Ukrainian Easter-egg decorating technique and wanted as much practice as possible, I chose to make the place cards for that year's event on eggshells. Each guest received a specially designed egg with their name on it, sitting in a napkin ring marking their spot at the table. To this day, some twenty years later, cousins, aunts, and uncles tell me they still have their egg.

For special events like weddings, birthdays, showers, births, and so on, a personalized egg makes a unique and charming gift. You can work out a meaningful pattern, such as a double wedding ring for an engaged couple, and integrate their names into the design. The possibilities are limitless—baby blocks for newborns...the wheat stalk (for abundance) for someone starting a new job...the schoolhouse pattern for a friend entering college or for a new teacher...holiday decorations of all kinds.

Eggs for new babies might incorporate the tumbling-block or baby-block design, borrowed from quilting, or such motifs as animals or rattles. For this one, I chose a turquoise and chartreuse color scheme over the traditional baby blues or pinks.

LAST WORDS

Once you've sampled the art, the craft, and the fun of egg decorating, the journey can take you anywhere. I wish you joy in your adventure.

An eggshell jewelry or keepsake box strikes me as one of the most elegant ways to make decorated eggs functional. For this one I chose the tumbling-blocks pattern.

Acknowledgments

I gratefully acknowledge all those who have contributed their work to this book, collectors who loaned back my work for this book, the wonderful people at Lark who made this all possible, my co-workers, and, most important, my family, who have helped me thrive through all of it:

Rachel Atkinson

Meredith Bernstein

Evan Bracken

Linda Bracken

Elizabeth Bullis-Wiese

Ellen and Paul Cahill

Donna Callaghan

Linda and Jon Carr

Lydia Chaves

Dorothy Discko

Marni-Rae Esposito

Susan Ferguson

Jodi Fisher

Elizabeth Fromentin

Vanessa Garnett

Leslie Gold

Andy Goodman

Anita Goodman

Cindy Grinnell

Elizabeth Hagyard

Rebecca Hudspeth

Dana Irwin

Claudia Kelly

Pat Klimaytis

Roberta Lombardino

Bobbe Needham

Carmen Picarello

Lindsey, Robert, and Laura Pollack

Joe Provey

Rob Pulleyn

Barbara Raho

Joseph Roll

Dr. Daniel Saracynski

Maria Saracynski

Kolene Spicher

Pat Talley

Elaine Thompson

Emily Trespas

Elizabeth Wheeler

Rachel Wheeler

Lubow Wolynetz

Paul Wirhun

I am grateful to these generous places of business in Asheville, North Carolina, for lending props for some of our photographs: Lexington Park Antiques, The Natural Home, and Preservation Hall (Architectural Salvage & Antiques).

For the photographs not taken by Evan Bracken, credit and thanks go to:

Donna Callaghan

David Egan

Susan Ferguson

Carmine Picarello

Joe Provey

Index

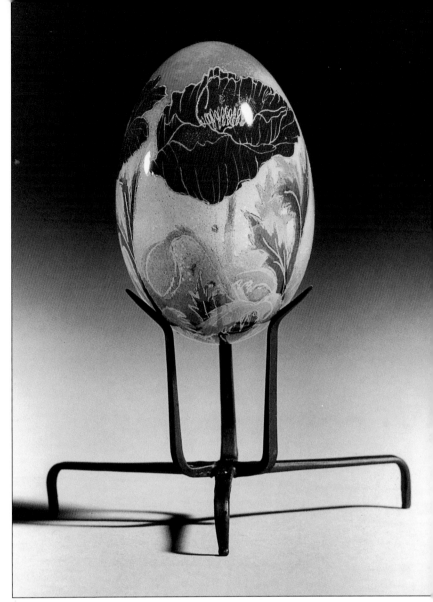

Poppy by Paul Wirhun